Presented To:

From:

Date:

All Scripture is given by inspiration of God, and is profitable for doctrine, for reproof, for correction, for instruction in righteousness, that the man of God may be complete, thoroughly equipped for every good work. 2 Timothy 3:16-17

Life Transforming
Bible Study

Life Transforming

Bible Study

How to Get God's Truth For Yourself

Kevin and Kathy Miiller

Copyright © 2017 Kevin and Kathy Miiller

All rights reserved. This book is protected by the copyright laws of the United States of America. This book may not be copied or reprinted for commercial gain or profit. Permission is granted to reprint the pdf version for personal use. As well, the use of short quotations or occasional page copying for personal or group study is permitted and encouraged. Emphasis (bold, underlined, and within parentheses) in Scripture quotations is author's own.

To request special permission or to contact the author, email info@knightsoftheking.com

Unless otherwise noted, Scripture quotations are from the New King James Version ® (NKJV) of the Holy Bible. Copyright © 1982 by Thomas Nelson. Used by permission. All rights reserved.

v11202017

ISBN-13: 978-1546438502

ISBN-10: 1546438505

Acknowledgements

We would like to thank Bob Spurlock (Wings of Calvary), Andy Hayner (Full Speed Impact Ministries), Anthony Tijerina (Be the Gospel), Carol Travis (Healing Nebraska), Dallas Buchfinck (MOR Ministries), Todd McNicholas, Garth Wiebe (wiebefamily.org), Lisa Scherbenske and Timothy Jorgensen (Spirit Life Training) for their contributions to this book. From teaching to consultations to editorial input, your knowledge, experience, diversity and encouragement were invaluable to us. Thank you!

We would also like to thank our children for their support and help in this endeavor. From your extra hugs to mac 'n cheese meals to many hours spent discussing and proofreading content, you have been a big part of making this publication possible. We love you more than words can express.

Contents

Introduction
Why Should I Study the Bible? 1
How to Use This Book 3
Quick Start Tips 5
Yes, YOU Can Understand the Bible 7

Chapter 1: Getting Started
Study with a Question in Mind 11
The Best Way to Read Scripture 13
The Power of Absolutes 15
Implied Absolutes Unleash Truth 18
Personalize, Amplify and Apply Scripture 19

Chapter 2: The Bigger Picture
Context is Key 23
Study the Same Story in a Different Book 26
Understand How Scripture Applies to You 30
Ask Questions. Lots of Questions 38
Where Should I Start? 40

Chapter 3: Getting the Right Mindset
Do You Really Believe the Bible is True? 43
Challenge What You Believe 48
Read Through the Lens of God's Nature and Character 49
How Do I Know What a Scripture Means? 52
How Well Do You Know the Bible? 53

Chapter 4: Relying on Him
- Prayer is Key 57
- Revelation from the Holy Spirit is Awesome 59
- Keep It Simple. Stop Searching for Hidden Meanings 64
- Don't Add Requirements 68
- Stop Reading Commentaries 70

Chapter 5: Getting to Know Your Bible
- Read A Good Translation 73
- Appreciate Your Bible's Notation 77
- The Secret about Chapter, Verse, and Punctuation 82

Chapter 6: Power Tools for Bible Study
- Some Favorite Bible Study Resources 87
- The Mighty Key Word Search 92
- Word Definitions Matter 95
- A Remarkably Easy Way to Study Using Biblical Greek and Hebrew 99
- What is a Lexicon? and Other Resource Definitions 103

Chapter 7: Putting It All Together
- Summary of Tips to Understand a Scripture 105
- Carol Travis — Preparing to Preach 108
- Kathy's Favorite — Short and Sweet 109
- Lisa Scherbenske — Studying Book by Book 111
- Todd McNicholas — Disciple Someone in How to Study the Bible 113
- Kevin's Favorite — New Testament Review 115
- Bob Spurlock — Understand the Old Testament 118

Chapter 8: Next Steps
- Making Disciples 121
- Closing Thoughts 125

Bibliography

Introduction

When I open a book, I often skip the introduction to get to the "good part," but in this case, I think you will be glad you started right here. To get the most out of the following chapters, we take a few minutes here to explain what is in this book, why you should read it and how it can revolutionize your life. We love to encourage people and this chapter does just that. I'm not very good at waiting to get to the good part, so we have put some great quick start tips right up toward the beginning to give you a taste of what is to come.

Why Should I Study the Bible?

This may sound like a radical concept, but we don't actually *have to* read the Bible. We don't have to have a devotional time or journal. We don't have to; WE GET TO!

Why should we study the Bible? Well, God told us to know and obey His commands, and to do that, we need to know what those commands are. It's more than that, though. Way more. Many Christians live defeated lives, hanging onto the hope of Heaven after they die, because they don't understand the benefits that we have as believers today. There are enormous benefits that Jesus paid for — things that seem too good to be true. We have seen many awesome miracles, as have many other believers in Jesus Christ just like us. Of course, the biggest miracle of all is the life-transforming power of God coming to live inside a person when they make Jesus the Lord of their life. These things are made possible because someone chose to find out what God said in the Bible and believe what it says.

The Bible says that Jesus came to give LIFE, and give LIFE in abundance. That's what it's all about. His life is here; it's now. It's transforming, energizing, joy and love-filled life. It's the heartbeat of our God. One time a friend and I were chatting and in a moment of vulnerability he stopped and looked right into my eyes. He said, "I've been a Christian most of my life but sometimes I wonder if God is real. How do I know?" To that, I said, "God is more real than you and me or anything we see in this world. And the reason I know that is because I have seen the heart of God through His Holy Spirit and His Word."

I know God, and He talks to me, but it wasn't always like that. I started with the same questions as my friend, but choosing to study and believe the Bible has been an absolute game-changer for us. It has transformed our lives, our marriage and our family. Better yet, it has impacted those that we touch because the stuff of God is contagious. Life begets life; life is a seed that spreads and grows and renews.

The Bible is at the center of the tangible connection we have with God, and it is never-changing. If you want to revolutionize your life, if you want to find passion and purpose and meaning in life, there is no better place to look. The Holy Spirit is waiting and hoping that you will take the step to dive in, put in the time and never give up. He wants to open God's words to you like you have never known before. If you are satisfied with your walk with God then this book isn't for you. However, if you want more, if you want to boost your understanding and revelation in God's Word, if you want to know and see more of the power of God in your life, then this book is for you.

Introduction

How to Use This Book

Welcome to *Life Transforming Bible Study*. This book was written for everyone who wants to get truth from the Bible. This includes not only those who are relatively new to Bible study but also for Bible study veterans who are interested in getting some fresh practical tips. We have been surprised to find that Bible study never gets old; in fact, it becomes more fascinating as time goes forward.

This book is not intended to be the end-all of Bible study guides. Instead of a deep dive into rigorous, scholarly Bible hermeneutics, our aim in this book is that you find the contents practical, helpful, inspiring and powerful. Some of the tips are so simple a child could perform them, yet so powerful even the most seasoned theologian can benefit.

Yes, I think you will find that you certainly can study the Bible for yourself and receive amazing revelation from the Holy Spirit. This book is filled with methods and tips that make time in the Bible exciting and fun. Scripture will revolutionize our lives if we let it. God's love is contagious and His promises are awesome, His commands are sure and the rewards are wonderful.

We (Kevin and Kathy) are passionate about advancing God's Kingdom around the world, and you are a very important part of that. We pray that you know more of God's heart through this book — that He wants you and needs you to be His ambassador in this world. Jesus came to give us life in abundance, and that is still His desire. When we take in God's truth, we are taking in His life. The Word is a seed, and it grows. As the seed matures we see the fruit come out as life in every area.

Feel free to read this book on your own or with a friend. It would be ideal for a Bible study group of any age to complete one or more sections followed by discussion. Our goal was to keep the contents simple enough for teens to understand. With lots of examples and thought-provoking questions, a youth group would find the methods and activities to be powerful training tools that are still engaging and fun.

Note: We have included a few examples that are still debated today. Our goal in this book is to offer helpful methods and techniques for Bible study, NOT to promote our doctrinal views. Because we feel that lots of examples make it easier to understand how these methods work, we have included many from our own study experience. You may agree or disagree with some of our conclusions, but in the end, it is up to you to "study out" each topic and get God's truth for yourself. God's truth is the same yesterday, today and forever.

You will notice that we have included some short stories from our own experiences with the owner's name beside it in square brackets (e.g., [Kevin]). Where the letter, "I" is used throughout the book, it could mean either Kevin or Kathy, since we both did plenty of writing. Toward the end, we have included a variety of sample Bible study methods to consider as you determine what works best for you. We pray that you find them helpful and inspirational.

We hope you connect with us at Knights of the King Ministries for more teaching, videos and encouragement.

Come visit us!

On Facebook:
https://www.facebook.com/KnightsOfTheKingMinistries

or online at: www.knightsoftheking.com

Quick Start Tips

The Bible is not like a novel that we read from front to back. Essentially, the Bible is a how-to-live-your-life manual, but it is not just a book about do's and don'ts. It is much, much more than that.

The Word of God begins with creation and tells God's love story to His people and His children (in which we are included). It includes the promises that He has made throughout history and His marvelous plan to conquer Satan and death, making a way for us to become His children and be forever connected and reconciled to Him! It tells us that our job here on earth is to advance His Kingdom, preach the Gospel and make disciples. The Bible reveals events that will happen when Jesus comes back to bring all of God's children home. My favorite part of the Bible includes all the promises and tools we have been given to do His work.

It is an awesome thought to consider how much truth is packed into the Bible; that a mind more brilliant than we can imagine has put His words onto paper through the writers chosen to record them. The best part is that He *wants* to communicate with us; He *wants* us to understand!

As we launch into the wonderful study methods and tools in this book, let's begin with a few quick start tips.

When reading the Bible:

- Pretend that you are reading each verse for the very first time. Do not assume that you already know what it says or what it means.
- Read each sentence slowly; don't rush. To better understand, we must take in every word.
- Read passages out loud. Make sure to speak every word.
- Play Scripture recordings wherever you are. While you sleep, drive, eat, work, clean the house or do chores, find creative ways to consume the Bible.
- Write Scripture passages that you want to ponder on pieces of paper, then tape* them in strategic places. Where do you look most often? Maybe the bathroom mirror, by the toilet, in the kitchen, on the cupboard/refrigerator, TV, light switch, on a

door or by a computer monitor? Purpose to read each Scripture out loud every time you see it throughout the day.

*Kathy's note: make sure that whatever surfaces you pick will not be damaged by tape.

> True story: at one point Kevin taped some verses to the ceiling fan blades above our bed. I would not recommend this because when we took off the tape it also took off the wood color. We certainly read them up there, though!

When Kevin and I were first married, he wasn't a vegetable fan. I think I inundated him with veggies in a way that sent him running for fast food. After a few years, he looked at me across the table and said, "You know, I'm really hungry for a big salad." He continued, "I guess after all this time I've gotten so used to eating this way that I actually crave vegetables."

The same is true for the Bible. It might seem slow or even unpleasant at first, but with regular time spent in God's Word we develop an appetite for it, look forward to study, and even crave time with God.

Introduction

YES, YOU CAN UNDERSTAND THE BIBLE

There is a belief among some followers of Jesus Christ that the Bible is confusing and mysterious. A sermon is delivered from the pulpit, complete with Greek and Hebrew words that we can't pronounce, much less understand. We hear about special *revelations* that people receive from God through the Bible and wish that we could hear from God, too. But when many open their Bibles they don't see those amazing truths revealed. It's just words on a page in a holy book. We read them and they're great, but we don't really grasp them. And we may wonder if we need more training, more time, more prayer, more…something.

Well, we are pleased to say that every believer in Jesus Christ, right now, no matter whether they became a follower of Jesus five minutes or fifty years ago, CAN know the Bible even more. Every person can receive truth from the Bible that they have never heard in a sermon or devotional book. God wants you to understand His Word and He's not hiding anything!

We know that God's plan is for us to understand the Bible for ourselves because we have been instructed to "preach the Gospel to every creature" (Mark 16:15). He also says that He has revealed His great mystery, which is "Christ in you, the hope of glory" (Colossians 1:27). In addition, He has given each person the "ministry of reconciliation" (2 Corinthians 5:18). What does all of this mean? It means that Christ is *in* us. That's His plan to spread the Gospel to every creature! We are to *reconcile* the world to God. That means our job is to bring other people to Jesus. How do we do that? By sharing and showing what God tells us in the Bible. And we don't even have to know much to be a powerful force used by God.

After you follow the practical steps in this book you will be amazed at how easy God has made it to get truth from the Bible. He is on our side; we just have to put in the time and be obedient. Keep knocking and never give up.

Matthew 7:7 — Ask, and it will be given to you; seek, and you will find; knock, and it will be opened to you.

In this book, we walk through simple, practical steps that, when applied, will leave you wide-eyed, full of joy and excitement about the Bible like you have never known before. Trust me, you won't be able to keep it to yourself.

Myth: God needs trained ministers, not me.

When Jesus was on earth He recruited His disciples from various walks of life. Some of them were fishermen by trade. These were not the highly-educated intellectuals of the day; they were the common folk. Jesus chose them to be the first to spread the Gospel. If He chose fishermen, we know that we don't need a college degree, certificate from Bible school, license or ordination to understand the Bible. The only thing we need is Him, and if we made Him Savior and Lord of our lives, He already lives inside us through His Holy Spirit.

The Holy Spirit is vital and He is amazing! The Holy Spirit is the key to the life and understanding that pours out of the Bible. He is the one who *reveals* God's Word to us, also known as *revelation*. In fact, He says that you already have the mind of Christ, whether you feel like it or not.

Yes, YOU have the mind of Christ. When God made you a new creation at the time you made Jesus your Lord and Savior, he placed His Holy Spirit inside you. Having His Spirit (the Holy Spirit) means that you have His mind and that you know ALL things (1 Corinthians 2:16 and 1 John 2:20). The knowledge and wisdom of God is in your spirit. The next step is to get this knowledge from your spirit into your mind. Study of the Bible and the Holy Spirit merge as a powerful team to get these godly truths from our spirit into our mind.

Why study the Bible? In a nutshell, the Bible is a straightforward guide to understanding God's Will and how to live life His way, because He knows what is best. As we study, our minds are changed to think the way God thinks, with His perspective. That's called *renewing our mind* (Romans 12:2). Just like the rudder of a boat or a horse being guided by the reigns of his rider, when our mind is in alignment with what God says, our lives follow suit. When we renew our minds, we start to change. We are no longer anxious, afraid, or sick. We have love, hope, direction and purpose for our lives. Best of all, we know our Father God's heart and His nature.

Introduction

Change how you think/change how you live

In this world we are bombarded by the earthly, physical way of thinking. Fear, lust, anger and sadness are trying to establish a place in our minds so that each time we encounter a situation, we respond in a worldly way (the Bible calls this *fleshly*). This is the way the enemy (the devil) wants us to think. It's a powerless, chaotic, hopeless and self-centered way of thinking. How we respond to a situation is a direct reflection of our perspective — our way of thinking. Peace and joy come when we see situations through God's lens, the Bible.

For example, imagine on a table before you are two pairs of sunglasses; one has red lenses and the other blue. Everything that we see in the world is tinted by the glasses we choose, and ultimately, those glasses dictate what happens in our lives. Here is the key: how we live, think and feel in our physical daily life in this world is based on what version of *truth* we accept. Do we accept God's truth or the enemy's version? Jesus said to *only believe*. What are we believing? How we perceive situations in life and what we believe has a huge impact on the actual physical reality we experience.

If God is for us, who can be against us?
Romans 8:31b

God's truth is still the ultimate truth whether we accept it or not. God's eternal life that He promised is not just in heaven. It's here right NOW. We live the life Jesus paid for, full of joy and peace as we choose to study and believe His Word, the Bible. It is definitely worth our time! As we learn from the Bible we understand that our Father God wants to bless and take care of us now and in the future.

"But I'm not sure what to study. Don't I have to wait for God to choose to teach me what I need to know?" Actually, no. The Holy Spirit is delighted to teach us whatever we want to know from God's Word, on any topic, as much as we want. We get to choose! The topic is up to you. Free yourself from worrying that God will be angry or offended if you don't constantly ask and wait for His direction in what to study. He is pleased when we decide to make time with Him and study His Word.

The Holy Spirit knows exactly what we need to learn and He will make a way to teach us, usually by creating a prompting or desire in us. Don't over-spiritualize it. When it comes to choosing what to study, ask God. If you don't get an answer, pick a topic and start. Just do it.

Before we begin, realize that one of the most common mistakes believers make is to study the Bible but not put it into practice. The Bible is clear that to truly understand the Bible, we need to hear it and then do it (James 1:22-25). For example, to really understand how to ride a bicycle, we don't stop with reading the instruction manual; we get on and try to pedal! Similarly, when a math teacher demonstrates solving a problem, we may know how to do it, but until we actually work through a problem ourselves we don't really own that knowledge. The Bible is understood and applied in much the same way.

Many people get stuck focusing on what they *don't* know. They try to learn more and more, thinking they will eventually feel they know enough to step out and put into practice what they have learned. The key is to stop focusing on what we don't know and decide to act on what we do know.

As we do the things that the Bible commands, our understanding of God's way of thinking — His truth — will grow dramatically. Our relationship with the Holy Spirit will flourish. We will receive new understanding of what the Bible means, acquire God's love for others like we never thought possible and develop a passion for knowing and doing His Word. Enough of the introduction. Let's go!

Chapter 1: Getting Started

This chapter contains some of the simplest yet most powerful techniques for really internalizing the Scripture we are reading. Engaging with the following examples will allow you to see Scripture in a totally new way.

STUDY WITH A QUESTION IN MIND

If you take nothing else away from this book I hope you get this one concept because it is a game changer: <u>study the Bible with a purpose</u>.

Bible study is so much more rewarding when we are looking for answers on a chosen subject. Do you have questions for God? Write down your questions, then read the Bible. Certain verses will seem to jump off the page. This was a key factor that changed my attitude from <u>feeling obligated to</u> read the Bible to <u>wanting to</u>. I felt hungry for answers.

In our opinion, our time spent in the Bible is most effective when we are actively seeking answers, with a mind open to God's truth. If God were physically sitting next to you right now, what would you ask Him? Write down these questions in a journal and start reading. I recommend taking a pocket-sized notebook and pen with you everywhere you go, because as you are actively seeking truth, the Holy Spirit will reveal it to you in many ways at various times of the day. Even though you may think you'll never forget what God told you, make sure to write everything down. Trust me, you will be glad you did!

James 1:5 — If any of you lacks wisdom, <u>let him ask of God, who gives to **all** liberally</u> and without reproach, and <u>it **will** be given to him</u>.

Expect that the Holy Spirit will draw your attention to the answers. He wants us to have the answers to our questions even more than we do! The Holy Spirit is excellent at His job of revealing the truth of the Bible.

John 16:13 — However, when He, the Spirit of truth, has come, He will guide you into all truth; for He will not speak on His own *authority*, but whatever He hears He will speak; and He will tell you things to come.

As the answers come, in your journal, write them down next to the original questions along with the date. This helps build faith! If the enemy ever tries to tell you that God doesn't care or that He doesn't answer, you will look back in this journal and remember that the God who created the entire universe loves you. He loves to talk with you and answer your questions, show you His will and reveal who He is.

Here's one of the most powerful things we have done as a couple: when God has answered a prayer, or we receive a miracle for ourselves or someone we are praying for, we write it down. This is one of the biggest devil lie-crushing exercises we can do! God told the Israelites to erect memorials so that they would never forget His faithfulness (for example, Joshua 4:20-24). We need to do that, too. Documenting God's work in our lives will serve as a testimony for our children and grandchildren.

A journal is a powerful reminder of the truth when the enemy tries to get us to doubt. Read through this list every year. Make it an annual day of remembering and giving glory to God! In fact, if you have the technology, you could put it in your calendar right now and set it to repeat and remind you every year on your birthday, the new year or a significant anniversary.

THE BEST WAY TO READ SCRIPTURE

In this section, we reveal a technique for reading the Bible that will revolutionize your understanding. There are two components. The first is one of the most difficult but effective *keys: SLOW DOWN.* Slowly read each word and give your mind time to digest what you are reading. The second component is to read OUT LOUD. Make certain to clearly say every word. <u>Combine the two and we have our game changing method for studying the Bible:</u> *read slowly, out loud*. I know this sounds simple, but you will be amazed at how this technique will revolutionize your Bible study time!

Experiment: Select a chapter in Ephesians or Colossians. Read the chapter the way that you normally do (for most people it is reading silently and quickly). While you read, in a notebook, write down what impacts you as you read it. Next, read the same chapter again, but this time read it slowly and out loud. Again, write down what impacts you as you read. My guess is that you will have many more notes the second time!

The Bible says we are to meditate on Scripture (Joshua 1:8). The word *meditate* means to focus our thoughts so we may understand something deeply. The Hebrew word(s) translated to the English *meditate* mean to ponder, murmur, mutter, study and speak. Notice that the practice of meditation does not merely involve spending time focusing and thinking; it involves speaking, too!

Often, we hear the concept of meditation likened to a cow or goat chewing its cud. They thoroughly chew and digest their food. When we slow down and take the time to focus on every word and speak it out loud, we are absorbing the truth much more easily. We can much more clearly understand each passage. What a difference! Reading it out loud forces us to not only slow down but also hear ourselves speak it. We see it, speak it and hear it. This gives us three times more impact than reading silently. If you want to take it a step further, write the Scripture, too!

Exercise

Here is a great technique for meditating on a verse. This technique is one of the simplest and most effective ways to get more out of Scripture.

1. Find a verse that you would like to understand even better or a promise that you wish to see in your life. We will use the first part of Acts 1:8 as an example below (see shaded area).
2. Slowly read the passage below out loud, emphasizing the first word (in **bold** text) by saying it louder than the others. After reading the first line, pause and reflect on its meaning.
3. Now repeat the passage, emphasizing the next word. Every time you come to a **bold** word, say it louder to emphasize it.
4. Continue repeating, emphasizing the next bold word until you have emphasized each word at least once.

But you shall receive power when the Holy Spirit has come upon you;

But **you** shall receive power when the Holy Spirit has come upon you;

But you **shall** receive power when the Holy Spirit has come upon you;

But you shall **receive** power when the Holy Spirit has come upon you;

But you shall receive **power** when the Holy Spirit has come upon you;

But you shall receive power **when** the Holy Spirit has come upon you;

But you shall receive power when **the** Holy Spirit has come upon you;

But you shall receive power when the **Holy** Spirit has come upon you;

But you shall receive power when the Holy **Spirit** has come upon you;

But you shall receive power when the Holy Spirit **has** come upon you;

But you shall receive power when the Holy Spirit has **come** upon you;

But you shall receive power when the Holy Spirit has come **upon** you;

But you shall receive power when the Holy Spirit has come upon **you**;

Did you notice how you could see a different facet of truth in this verse each time you emphasized a different word? This is also a powerful exercise to memorize a verse in the Bible, glean truth from it and activate it in our lives.

The Power of Absolutes

Let's do an experiment. Glance down and read this passage from 2 Peter 3:9 quickly.

2 Peter 3:9 — The Lord is not slack concerning *His* promise, as some count slackness, but is longsuffering toward us, not willing that any should perish but that all should come to repentance.

Now read the same verse below, but this time read out loud slowly, speaking every word. Put extra emphasis on each underlined word and pause slightly.

2 Peter 3:9 — The Lord is not slack concerning *His* promise, as some count slackness, but is longsuffering toward us, not willing that <u>any</u> should perish but that <u>all</u> should come to repentance.

Did you pay careful attention to the underlined words, *any* and *all*? These are ABSOLUTE words, meaning that there are NO exceptions. The Bible explodes with meaning when we take notice of absolute words. When God said *all*, He meant *ALL*. Once we realized that, it was life-changing!

Some of the absolute words are:

| All | Always | Any | Every | Everything | Only |
| No | Nothing | Shall | Whatever | Whoever | Will |

A very simple but valuable practice is to simply underline or circle the absolute words in a passage you are studying. If you have never given yourself permission to write in your Bible, consider that permission granted! Bookstores often sell highlighters and pens specially designed for taking notes on the thin pages of a Bible. Something wonderful happens when we draw attention to these absolute words because they make us realize the enormity of what God has said. He makes no exceptions, there's no fine print, and He doesn't back out of His promises.

Here is another passage. This time, locate and underline the absolute words.

Luke 10:19 — Behold, I give you the authority to trample on serpents and scorpions, and over all the power of the enemy, and nothing shall by any means hurt you

In Luke 10:19 we see the absolute words, *all, nothing, any* and *shall*. That means that Jesus has given believers authority over *all* (every single bit) of the enemy's power. Furthermore, *nothing* (not even one little thing) shall hurt us. We cannot be hurt by any means of the enemy. What powerful promises!

Luke 10:19 was revolutionary to us when we stopped to think about what it truly says. If you are having difficulty believing this verse, we suggest looking at what happened to Paul in Acts 28:3-6. This passage demonstrates Luke 10:19 in action.

Let's try one more passage. Mark 11:22-24 tells us how to get answers to prayer. In the passage below, circle all the absolute words. Consider the power of each absolute word.

> **Mark 11:22-24** — ²² So Jesus answered and said to them, "Have faith in God. ²³ For assuredly, I say to you, whoever says to this mountain, 'Be removed and be cast into the sea, and does not doubt in his heart, but believes that those things he says will be done, he will have whatever he says. ²⁴ Therefore I say to you, whatever things you ask when you pray, believe that you receive them, and you will have them."

The absolute words, *will, whoever, and whatever* appear in this passage. Through these words, God is telling us that if anyone makes a declaration (statement or command) and does not doubt, but believes, it will happen. When we apply this to our own lives, we know that for anything we ask, we only need to believe that we have already received them and we are guaranteed to have them.

> [Kathy] I think that for many, biblical absolutes are difficult to believe because when they sink into our minds, we are literally awestruck. Most of the time we pass over absolute words with little thought, but when we stop to appreciate what God has said in His Word, it can be difficult to grasp. We need assistance from the Holy Spirit to really internalize each truth. At times, I sit and stare at the page, wondering if I will be able to grasp the awesomeness of what God has promised. That's where revelation from the Holy Spirit comes in.

If we do not respect the absolute words of the Bible by taking them literally, we water down God's Word. The world we live in likes shades of grey, with sayings like, "there are no absolutes." But the God who created the universe goes by absolute right and wrong, truth and lies, and light and darkness. Imagine if gravity was in effect only some of the time! We can count on God's physical and spiritual laws being absolutely true, all the time.

Before Jesus came to earth, He was known as *The Word of God*. Jesus knows communication better than anyone. We can rest assured that when He says ALL, He means ALL. When we believe what He said, His promises start to become reality in our lives.

IMPLIED ABSOLUTES UNLEASH TRUTH

After we understand that God is a God of absolutes, then two things will start to happen.

1. We will notice many of the absolutes in the Bible and
2. We will begin to understand that sometimes absolutes are not explicitly stated in Scripture. They are *implied*.

Let's explore what implied absolutes are and why they are so important to develop rich insight into God's Word. Read 1 John 1:9.

1 John 1:9 — If we confess our sins, He is faithful and just to forgive us *our* sins and to cleanse us from all unrighteousness.

At first glance, we see the absolute word, *all*. However, there are other *implied* absolutes. We look at not only what the passage says, but also what it does not say. Let's explain.

We know that when God says something, He means it. With God, exceptions are almost non-existent. Furthermore, after we grasp the nature and character of God, we can appreciate what He is truly saying by adding the implied absolute words. Following is the same verse with the implied absolutes added in parentheses.

1 John 1:9 (expanded version) — If we confess our sins, He is (always and forever) faithful and (always) just to (completely) forgive us (all) *our* sins (every single time) and to (completely) cleanse us from all unrighteousness (and if we are cleansed from unrighteousness, we are left with only righteousness).

We never want to add any manmade requirements or regulations for receiving God's promises that He did not add. That would introduce error. Looking for implied absolutes allows us to further expose and emphasize the truth that is already there because we understand who He is. If there are no exceptions listed, then we know that it is an absolute truth.

Read the expanded version of 1 John 1:9 again. Isn't that amazing? The truth in this verse comes alive as we see God's grace and love toward us in this passage. His nature and character is evident by what He has done, and who He has made us to be. What is God's plan and will for us according to 1 John 1:9? Righteousness. He is faithful to cleanse us from all unrighteousness and to make us spotless. Next time you study, look for implied absolutes!

Personalize, Amplify and Apply Scripture

This section isn't as much about how to study Scripture, but how to internalize what we have studied. When I study a topic, I often come across Scripture that I struggle to believe. At first I didn't want to admit it, but as I have gone along I realize that this is an opportunity to renew my mind to God's way of thinking.

Believing what the Bible says is the result of a choice. Our belief is based on our choice to trust God, not necessarily because we have revelation from the Holy Spirit in every area. When I check in the far corner of my mind, I sometimes find a part of me that is skeptical and doubting. For example, when we read a passage like Luke 10:19, it might be a stretch for us to believe that nothing can hurt us. Rather than hoping to believe it someday, I have learned that taking action to believe this Scripture produces dramatic results. God's Word is His pledge. He loves to use Scripture when He talks with us, and He loves it when we use Scripture when we talk with Him.

The aim is to reprogram our thinking. We take portions of our thinking that do not line up with God's Word and align them, similar to the way a chiropractor adjusts the body. Once we have aligned our thoughts consistently for long enough, Godly thinking in that area becomes automatic.

The following is a powerful technique that has transformed me. Remember that we are going to internalize and activate a biblical truth that we *want* to believe. Whether we believe it right now or not is irrelevant. Following are the basic steps.

1. Identify the verse (or portion thereof) that you want to believe more.
2. Identify the principle behind that piece and say it in your own words, applying it to yourself, a situation or your life.
3. Turn it into a conversation with God. Expand, amplify and apply the principle to other areas, focusing on any explicit or implied absolutes. If it is a promise of God to you, state that fact. If it is a command, state how you will obey in your life.

We think, then we verbalize what we are thinking. All the while, we hear ourselves speaking. Combined, these steps change and train our minds. We are literally brainwashing ourselves. I don't know about you, but washing my brain with God's Word sounds like a great idea!

Let's walk through an example.

> **Luke 10:19** — Behold, I give you the authority to trample on serpents and scorpions, and over all the power of the enemy, and <u>nothing shall by any means hurt you.</u>

The last portion of that Scripture has been especially meaningful for me, because this world tells us that everything can hurt us. That's not what Jesus said! When we read this Scripture, we see that Jesus is talking to His disciples, and that there appears to be no other requirement to receive this promise other than to be Jesus' disciple and to know that we have been given Jesus' authority over the enemy's ability. We are Jesus' disciples, right? So here is how this portion of Scripture could be turned into a statement of faith in this promise. Read this statement loud and strong.

"Jesus said in Luke 10:19 that nothing would by any means hurt me. That means that no demon or situation can hurt me. I am free to go about my life, doing God's work with no fear because He said that there is nothing that can hurt me."

Here's another example. In John 14:12, Jesus said that the works He did we will do also, and even greater works. We know that when Jesus went to the Father, He sent back the Holy Spirit to live inside every believer. He is what makes these works possible.

> **John 14:12** — Most assuredly, I say to you, he who believes in Me, the works that I do he will do also; and greater *works* than these he will do, because I go to My Father.

Here is an example of how I would personalize, amplify and apply some of the principles in this verse. We will turn this one into a prayer, or statement of faith we make to God.

"Father God, you said that the works Jesus did, I would also do. Jesus went to the Father to send the Holy Spirit to all believers. I am a believer, so I have all I need to do the works Jesus did. Jesus healed the sick, He raised the dead, He fed the hungry, and He preached the Gospel. I can do all those things and more because the Holy Spirit lives in me. You (God) said that I <u>shall</u> do those works. I believe on Jesus and that is the only requirement to unlock this promise. I will trust, obey and do what you are telling me to do in John 14:12."

We can now add additional Scriptures to expand even more. Notice that we are speaking by faith using Jesus' example of speaking those things that are not as though they were. The final step is to not only speak about these commands and promises but do what God says we should do. When we lay hands on the sick, they do recover.

"Father God, I know the Holy Spirit abides and lives in me. You said you would never leave me or forsake me so while I do the works Jesus did, I never need to worry about whether you are there. The Holy Spirit is in me all the time. He stays with me forever and I trust Him to lead and guide me into all truth. Father, your Word says that I can do all things through Christ who strengthens me. I have been given everything I need to do every good work. I do all the works Jesus did and more. You said that believers shall lay their hands on the sick and they will recover. I am a believer, I lay my hands on the sick, and they do recover. I may not have seen it yet, but I know your Word is true and I believe your promises. Any thought in my mind that does not agree with the Bible is a lie and I refuse to believe it. Everything You say in the Bible is true and I choose to believe it no matter what. God's Word is forever settled in Heaven and it does not change. What was true then is true now and you have given me authority over all the ability of the enemy and nothing shall hurt me. Not even one little thing can hurt me while I go about doing the works that Jesus did. I do spread the good news of the Gospel and today I will obey you by loving you and loving people. All these things are possible because your Holy Spirit is with me. Amen."

Do you see how we combined several biblical principles in Scripture, personalized them, amplified and applied them to life? We state God's truth as fact, and in doing so, we begin to believe it more and more. The Bible is very clear that there is power in our words. Jesus used words to work miracles most of the time. In fact, He was called *The Word*. Without a doubt, there is power in the name of Jesus!

The more we repeat and apply Scripture, the more our mind is renewed to God's way of thinking. This process changes what we say, hear and think, which changes our beliefs and by faith we get the things we are trusting God for. We speak it, then we act on the commands and promises of God and our faith and trust grow. It is a cycle that bears an abundance of fruit.

We have done this activity alone and with others and it is powerful. You only need a piece of one verse to start and it will grow from there. Here's the goal: when a thought pops in your head that does not line up with the Bible, you will remember the biblical statements you made and quickly adjust your thinking in line with truth.

Someone asked me one time, "How do you know when you've done it enough?" I thought about it for a while, and basically said, "You have done it (biblical confessions) enough when you don't have to try anymore in that area. Biblical thinking in that area becomes automatic." As a younger person, when we first learn to read, ride a bike or drive a car, we must think about every step, but the more we do those things, the more automatic they become. When we have confessed God's Word enough, we don't have to stop and intentionally correct bad thinking, we think in line with the Bible without even trying. We don't have to fight bad thoughts in that area anymore because they simply fall away.

Initially I did this exercise on my own a lot. By a lot, I mean several hours a day. I would even sit in the parking lot at work for five to ten minutes before going in, then over my lunch break I would go out to my car and confess some more. It really helped to listen to Scripture on an mp3 player wherever I went, because it gave me more ammunition to change my thinking. Essentially, I was detoxifying my mind. The fastest way to detoxify is to consistently immerse ourselves in clean, biblical thinking and cut out worldly influences as much as possible.

There are a number of ministries that provide topical Scripture confessions. They are available in a variety of formats, including written, audio, video and app, but the best is always selecting meaningful Scripture and writing your own. Consistent confessions of Scripture will help you personalize, amplify, and apply it, which is guaranteed to change your life.

Chapter 2: The Bigger Picture

In this chapter, we explore how broadening our focus allows us to see how a small portion of Scripture fits into the whole so we can accurately understand it. This bigger picture adds great depth to Bible study.

CONTEXT IS KEY

We often hear that, to know the Bible, we need to be able to understand it *in context*. Reading the Bible in context means that we don't simply take one verse, or part of a verse, and draw conclusions from it. To understand it correctly we need to know what the verse is talking about in the scope of the entire passage.

It is almost impossible to really understand a verse by reading it on its own. Studying a single verse without reading the other Scripture before and after is comparable to watching a one-minute clip from a movie. From the movie clip, we have an idea about what is happening, but when the clip is taken in context of the whole movie, our understood meaning is richer and more accurate.

Taking Scripture out of context can have dire consequences and can completely derail a believer. Some people have built entire organizations (cults) upon a small piece of Scripture taken out of context. We are all growing, and we will make mistakes interpreting Scripture, but if we make sure to simply read a verse in context, we will dramatically reduce misinterpretation. Reading in context is easy! Simply read the verse in light of the other verses around it.

To begin understanding the context of a verse:
1. Read several verses before and after the verse in question. Start with three verses before and three after.
2. To gain an even better understanding of the passage in context, expand the reading area to the entire chapter the verse appears in.
3. For even more clarity, read the chapter before, the chapter that contains the verse, and the chapter after.

Example: Romans 8:28a is a verse quoted by (or about) people who are going through difficulty.

Romans 8:28a — And <u>we know that all things work together for good</u>

I have heard people quote this portion of Romans 8:28a, followed by the implication that God caused or allowed this difficulty so that He can turn it into something good later. This is not what everyone thinks, but Romans 8:28 is an example of a verse commonly taken out of context.

Now let's look at the entire verse.

Romans 8:28 — And we know that all things work together for good to those who love God, <u>to those who are the called according to *His* purpose</u>.

The second half of the verse gives a clearer picture. We see that Romans 8:28 only applies to those who *love God*. For people who have not made Jesus their Lord and Savior, this verse does not apply.

Next, we expand our reading to three verses before and three after. Read slowly, giving the Holy Spirit time to speak to you about what this passage is saying.

Romans 8:25-31 — [25] But if we hope for what we do not see, we eagerly wait for *it* with perseverance. [26] Likewise the Spirit also helps in our weaknesses. For we do not know what we should pray for as we ought, but the <u>Spirit Himself makes intercession</u> for us with groanings which cannot be uttered. [27] Now He who searches the hearts knows what the mind of the Spirit *is,* <u>because He makes intercession for the saints according to *the will of* God</u>.

28 And we know that all things work together for good to those who love God, to those who are the called according to *His* purpose. 29 For whom He foreknew, He also predestined *to be* conformed to the image of His Son, that He might be the firstborn among many brethren. 30 Moreover whom He predestined, these He also called; whom He called, these He also justified; and whom He justified, these He also glorified. 31 What then shall we say to these things? If God *is* for us, who *can be* against us?

What did the Holy Spirit show you about this passage? When I read Romans 8:28 in context, I see that things work together for good for believers because the Spirit is praying for us according to God's Will. He does this for those who are the called according to His purpose. What is His purpose? To be conformed to the image of Jesus.

In short, Romans 8:28 does not sound like a verse to give comfort to those who are going through a tragedy, it is a victorious verse for those who are actively pursuing God's plan for their lives. We see in verse 26 that God realizes we sometimes don't know how to pray, but He is working hard for our good because His Will is for us to live every day focused on accomplishing His mission, not worrying about anything that would stand in our way. I love verse 31, that summarizes it by saying, "If God is for us, who can be against us?" Amen!

STUDY THE SAME STORY IN A DIFFERENT BOOK

When a crime occurs, the assigned detective interviews everyone who was at the scene to get the complete story. We have the same opportunity to do this in the Bible. Sometimes the same story is written by different authors in different books*. These are called *parallel* passages, and they occur in the Gospels (Matthew, Mark, Luke and John). If we carefully read every account of the same story, we get the most accurate picture of what happened. Like a detective, we then make conclusions on our findings.

*Note: Some Bibles will mark parallel verses (different accounts of the same story) with notation such as a superscript letter (e.g. [a]).

Here's an example. We have heard it said that "Jesus could not heal in His hometown because of the people's unbelief." This statement is based on an incorrect interpretation of an account from Jesus' ministry.

This story may be read in two different places in the Bible (two *parallel passages*). From these two writers, Matthew and Mark, we get two perspectives and a clearer understanding of what happened that day.

> **Matthew 13:54-58** — [54] When He had come to His own country, He taught them in their synagogue, so that they were astonished and said, "Where did this *Man* get this wisdom and *these* mighty works? [55] Is this not the carpenter's son? Is not His mother called Mary? And His brothers James, Joses, Simon, and Judas? [56] And His sisters, are they not all with us? Where then did this *Man* get all these things?" [57] So they were offended at Him. But Jesus said to them, "A prophet is not without honor except in his own country and in his own house." [58] Now He did not do many mighty works there because of their unbelief.

Notice in Matthew 13:54-58 above, Jesus did not do <u>many</u> mighty works due to the people's unbelief. Following is a parallel passage detailing the same account in Mark.

> **Mark 6:1-5** — [1] Then He went out from there and came to His own country, and His disciples followed Him. [2] And when the Sabbath had come, He began to teach in the synagogue. And many hearing *Him* were astonished, saying, "Where *did* this Man *get* these things? And what wisdom *is* this which is given to

Him, that such mighty works are performed by His hands! ³ Is this not the carpenter, the Son of Mary, and brother of James, Joses, Judas, and Simon? And are not His sisters here with us?" So they were offended at Him. ⁴ But Jesus said to them, "A prophet is not without honor except in his own country, among his own relatives, and in his own house." ⁵ Now He could do no mighty work there, except that He laid His hands on a few sick people and healed *them.*

In Mark 6:1-5, notice that Jesus did no mighty works <u>except</u> that He laid His hands on a few sick people and healed them. When we compare the two, Matthew's account states that Jesus did only a few mighty works but Mark is more specific, stating that the only mighty work Jesus did was to heal the sick people.

Let's go back to the original statement that we have heard, "Jesus could not heal in his hometown because of the people's unbelief." This statement appears to be a piece from each of the two accounts (Matthew and Mark) twisted in a way that delivers a false image of what happened. We know that this statement is false because Jesus *did* heal. It says that he laid His hands on a *few* sick people and healed them. When we look at the same story told in Matthew and Mark, we are letting Scripture verify itself. Where there is ambiguity, we look to the parallel passage to clarify.

There are still a few questions that these two passages do not answer directly, such as, "Did Jesus heal ALL the sick people in His hometown or was He unable to heal some of them?" and "Why did He only heal a few people?" We can take this study to the next level by using a few more techniques. In essence, we are going to let Scripture verify itself by looking at the pattern and style of the writers to propose some answers to these questions.

First, let's address the question, "Did Jesus heal ALL the sick people in his hometown or was He unable to heal some of them?" To do this, we look at how the writers (Matthew and Mark) addressed similar situations in which Jesus was healing people. Throughout Matthew, Mark and the other Gospels, all the accounts which detail Jesus' healing miracles have something in common. Look through the Gospels for healing stories and you will see statements like "He (Jesus) healed *all*," "healing *every*," "healed their sick," "He healed them," "He laid His hands on *every one* of them and healed them," "they were healed," and "healed those who had need." What do all of these stories have in common? We never see a record of Jesus unable to heal someone. He always healed them all. This is Jesus' pattern of ministry as recorded by the writers.

I strongly encourage you to look for yourself. Jesus always healed everyone who came to Him all the time. Let's go back to the original topic in Mark again.

Mark 6:5 — ⁵ Now He could do no mighty work there, except that He laid His hands on a few sick people and healed *them*.

We not only look at what this passage says, but also what it does not say. In Mark 6:5, it does not say that Jesus healed a few *of* the sick people. It says that Jesus only laid His hands on a few sick people, but those people He touched were healed.

Our next question is compelling: "Why did Jesus only heal a few people?" It is safe to say that only a few sick people were healed, but why? Was the town just unusually healthy? I don't think that was the case. I believe that part of the confusion about Jesus' ability to heal in His hometown is because we *assume* that multitudes were present like they usually were when Jesus went somewhere. Let's look for more patterns in Matthew and Mark.

Each of the Gospel writers gave specific details about Jesus' miraculous ministry. When we read about the times people gathered to hear Jesus, we see the word *multitude* used to describe how many people came to hear Him in Matthew and Mark. Apparently, there were *multitudes* that came to Jesus a lot. *Multitude* is used in 47 verses in Matthew and in 25 verses in Mark.

Just for fun, let's get an estimation of the number of people they considered to be a *great multitude*. To do this, we again use the parallel passages of the same stories. In Matthew 14:13-21 and Mark 6:30-44 the *great multitudes* that were fed included 5,000 men besides women and children. In Matthew 15:29-39 it says the *great multitude* that was fed was 4,000 and Mark 8:1-8 states that the same *great multitude* was 4,000 men besides women and children. That's A LOT of people!

Following is an example from Mark. Notice how this passage describes the crowd size and the number of people who received healing.

Mark 3:7-10 — ⁷ But Jesus withdrew with His disciples to the sea. And a great <u>multitude</u> from Galilee followed Him, and from Judea ⁸ and Jerusalem and Idumea and beyond the Jordan; and those from Tyre and Sidon, a great <u>multitude</u>, when they heard how many things He was doing, came to Him. ⁹ So He told His disciples that a small boat should be kept ready for Him because of the <u>multitude</u>, lest they should crush Him. ¹⁰ For He <u>healed many</u>, so that as many as had afflictions pressed about

A <u>multitude</u> came, and <u>many</u> were healed. However, we never see the term, *multitude* used in either the Matthew or Mark account of Jesus healing in His hometown. Do we have reason to believe that only a few sick people came to Jesus in His hometown, and that all were healed? I believe that we do.

We don't know the exact number that came to Jesus, so we cannot make a concrete judgement about how many came to Him, but we also cannot assume that Jesus was unable to heal. The Bible never states that Jesus was unable to heal someone for any reason.

The last question we ask is, "WHY were there only a few people who came to hear and see Jesus in His hometown?" Usually, everywhere Jesus went, huge crowds followed Him.

From both accounts of this story we know that people knew Jesus' parents, brothers and sisters. Because they were familiar with Jesus' family, they did not believe that Jesus was anything special. They could not understand how Jesus had gained this wisdom and performed miracles with His own hands. The people from His hometown were offended at Him (did not believe what He said, did or who He was) so they did not come to Him.

Jesus laid His hands on a few sick people and healed them (Mark 6:5), so Jesus <u>did</u> heal amid their unbelief. Because many in His hometown did not believe who Jesus was and come to Him to get healed, Jesus only did a few mighty works by laying hands on the sick people that came.

In this section, we discussed how to look at parallel accounts of the same story in the Gospels. We also showed how some questions that are not answered directly can be investigated by looking at patterns in the writings. This isn't difficult, but we must be willing to put in the time. With a quick search, you can find many websites which list the references for all the parallel passages in the Gospels. Your Bible may also note any parallel passages with special notation within the story.

Understand How Scripture Applies to You

The Bible is comprised of several types of books. Some are books of the law (think of Moses and the Ten Commandments), some prophecy, some are historical accounts, some are letters (known as epistles) and so on. The books from Genesis to Malachi comprise the Old Testament and Matthew through Revelation are the New Testament. From Genesis to Revelation, the Bible is somewhat (but not exactly) in historical order.

Knowing the general events within the culture, country, and world at the time a book of the Bible was written gives us vital insight into what the writer is saying and why. Following are a few of the largest, most impactful biblical events throughout the world's history (in order).

Old Testament (Milestones)
- Creation (Genesis 1)
- Fall of Mankind, Sin Entered the World (Genesis 3)
- God's Covenant with Abraham (Genesis 17)
- Moses is given the Law (Exodus 20)

New Testament (Timeframes)
- The Life and Ministry, Death & Resurrection of Jesus Christ (Matthew 1-Acts 1)
- New Covenant was Established & Holy Spirit Sent to All Believers (all books Acts 2 through Jude) ← **We are here**. These books particularly apply to all those living today.
- Anti-Christ & Jesus' Return (Revelation)

Usually, it's not important to know *precisely* when a book of the Bible was written, but it is *critical* to know the basic timeframe. In other words, when we are reading, we consider the biblical events listed above and ask ourselves which timeframe that Scripture was written in. Let me explain why this is so important.

In the biblical timeframes list, notice that the second New Testament timeframe is the period *after* the Holy Spirit was sent to all believers. This portion of the Bible is particularly important to us because you and I are living in the time of God's New Covenant right now. Essentially, this means that the contents of Acts 2 through Jude especially apply to believers living today. Let's explore what that means.

Leading up to Acts 2, when we look at the Old Testament from Genesis through the New Testament Gospels, we see the beginning of humanity, God's mighty works, historical accounts, laws given by God to His chosen people, poetry, prophecies and much more. Sometimes, people read the Bible from beginning to end just as they would read a novel, not understanding that the earlier portions do not apply to them in the same way as they did to the people who lived during that time period.

For example, God gave numerous, very specific laws to the Israelites with details about how to handle all sorts of situations. There are consequences for sinful actions, special cleansings, and apparel and dietary laws that apply to very specific situations. We even see highly detailed directions for priests who are offering sacrifices to God. These are not rules that we have been taught to follow today. Why? Because those rules were written for God's people who were under a different covenant than we are today.

Today we are under the New Covenant. What is a covenant? God made several covenants (a contract, agreement, or promise) throughout the world's history, and these covenants coincide with the requirements and blessings God has established for those participating in those covenants. The exciting part is that God has said that the New Covenant (the covenant believers benefit from today) is a better covenant with better promises. This covenant affects everything – even our relationship with God. Finding out what God did for believers in this New Covenant is absolutely life-altering!

God gave the promise of the New Covenant to Abraham and his future offspring (Jesus) when Jesus completed His mission of dying on the cross and paying sin's penalty for all of humanity. The New Covenant then became available to all who believe in Jesus. Because Jesus satisfied the criteria for the New Covenant, mankind cannot break the covenant the way Adam did. However, believers still benefit from this covenant through eternal salvation, promises of the Kingdom and the availability of the Holy Spirit in a way never known before.

How can we learn more about what the New Covenant means for our lives? The Old Testament gives the promise and some details of the coming New Covenant, but to get a solid understanding, begin by reading what Jesus said about the Kingdom in the Gospels. As you read the Gospels and beyond, take note of all references to God's covenants and what each entails. It is truly remarkable. In fact, if you have never studied the New Covenant, we highly recommend it.

How does the New Covenant change how we read the Bible? Well, in the Old Testament, the Holy Spirit was very active, but people in general did not have the availability of God's anointing (the Holy Spirit) for everyone all the time. We see an example in Psalm 103:7, where God revealed His acts to Israel, but His ways to Moses.

Psalm 103:7 — ⁷ He (the LORD) made known his ways unto Moses, his acts unto the children of Israel.

God doesn't limit His contact with us through a prophet, the Ark of the Covenant or the Temple's Holy of Holies – He has completely reconciled mankind to Himself by recreating the spirit and making His home in every person who accepts Jesus' free gift. We don't have to worry that He will come and go on a whim. The Bible says that He abides (lives and dwells) in us.

The New Covenant gave rise to a whole new way of living and thinking for believers. It's a mindset we must have when we read the Bible so we know *how* a passage applies to us. To do this, we need to know the covenant that was in place for the biblical timeframe we are reading.

Let's look at an example showing how things have changed throughout biblical timeframes. To do this, we consider several passages from different biblical eras (as given in the beginning of this section), from earlier in history to more current. First, read Isaiah 5:8-9. Isaiah is a book of prophecy in the Old Testament, written long before Jesus came.

Isaiah 55:8-9 — ⁸ "For My thoughts *are* not your thoughts, Nor *are* your ways My ways," says the Lord. ⁹ "For *as* the heavens are higher than the earth, <u>So are My ways higher than your ways, And My thoughts than your thoughts.</u>"

This passage is quoting what God was saying through Isaiah, basically stating that we can never expect to understand God's ways with our little human brains. How could mankind even come close to His wisdom and knowledge? When we read Isaiah 55:8-9, we get a picture of how brilliant and awesome God is. At the same time, it emphasizes the disconnect between God and mankind, both physically and mentally.

Next, we read from the Gospel of John. This book contains stories and teachings given during the life and ministry of Jesus. Even though the Gospels are in the New Testament, technically they are not in the New Covenant timeframe because Jesus had not yet fulfilled His mission. In John 16:12-13 Jesus was telling His disciples what was to come.

John 16:12-13 — ¹² "I still have many things to say to you, <u>but you cannot bear *them* now</u>. ¹³ However, <u>when He, the Spirit of truth, has come, He will guide you into all truth</u>; for He will not speak on His own *authority*, but whatever He hears He will speak; and He will tell you things to come."

During Jesus' ministry time, His life was a demonstration of how the Kingdom of God operated on earth. God has established spiritual laws that benefit only those who have accepted Jesus Christ, including the gift of the Holy Spirit (the Spirit of truth). In John 16:12, Jesus said He wanted to share even more things with the disciples, but they would not be able to bear them until they had the Holy Spirit. Before they received the Holy Spirit, their thoughts and understanding were more limited to their carnal (earthly) thinking. The Holy Spirit would not be available in the way Jesus describes until Acts 2 after Jesus ascended into Heaven.

Finally, let's look at passages in 1 Corinthians and 1 John, which occurred after Jesus ascended and sent the Holy Spirit. This is during the timeframe after the New Covenant was enacted. In this Scripture, we see that the Holy Spirit makes a big difference in our ability to comprehend the things of God. While you read, keep in mind that this is the era we live in!

1 Cor 2:11-16 — ¹¹ For what man knows the things of a man except the spirit of the man which is in him? Even so <u>no one knows the things of God except the Spirit of God</u>. ¹² Now <u>we have received</u>, not the spirit of the world, but <u>the Spirit who is from God, that we might know the things that have been freely given to us by God</u>. ¹³ These things we also speak, not in words which man's wisdom teaches but which <u>the Holy Spirit teaches, comparing spiritual things with spiritual</u>. ¹⁴ But the natural man does not receive the things of the Spirit of God, for they are foolishness to him; nor can he know *them*, because they are spiritually discerned. ¹⁵ But he who is spiritual judges all things, yet he himself is *rightly* judged by no one. ¹⁶ For "who has known the mind of the LORD that he may instruct Him?" <u>But we have the mind of Christ</u>.

1 John 2:20 — ²⁰ But <u>you have an anointing</u> from the Holy One, and <u>you know all things</u>.

And finally, 1 John 2:27:

1 John 2:27 — ²⁷ <u>But the anointing which you have received from Him abides in you</u>, and you do not need that anyone teach you; but <u>as the same anointing teaches you concerning all things, and is true, and is not a lie, and just as it has taught you, you will abide in Him</u>.

In 1 Corinthians 2, we see that the Spirit of God knows all things, and that we have received the Holy Spirit so that we might know the things of God. In verse 16, it goes on to say that we have the mind of Christ. We see more on this topic in 1 John 2:20, which says that we know all things. How can this be?

When we are saved, we become a new creation. According to 1 John 2:27, we received the anointing, who *is* the Holy Spirit. We are joined to Him and in union with Him (vs. 27, "you will <u>abide</u> in Him"). The Holy Spirit has all of God's knowledge and was sent to teach us all things. As a result, we now can understand the things of God because we have the mind of Christ.

The anointing we have been given (the Holy Spirit) means that we can know ALL THINGS in our spirit. We must move that knowledge from our spirit into our natural mind.

Looking back, do you see the sequential change from Isaiah, to John, to 1 Corinthians, and to 1 John?

- ➢ In Isaiah (the Old Testament), it says that man cannot understand God's thoughts and ways.

- ➢ Next, in the Gospels (John) during Jesus' ministry, He told the disciples they couldn't handle all the spiritual truth He wanted to tell them at that point, but when they received the Holy Spirit they would be able to.

- ➢ Then in 1 Corinthians and 1 John, after the Holy Spirit was given to believers, it says that we can now understand the things of God because we have the mind of Christ. Because of the New Covenant, we can have the Holy Spirit living (abiding) inside us, and because we are in union with Him, we know all things in our spirit.

This is only one example of how things are different for believers now, and it is key. Holy Spirit changed everything. God's goal was "Christ in you, the hope of glory" (Colossians 1:27).

Were all the things that happened before the cross important? Definitely! We still benefit from promises, wisdom, stories of faith, and commands given in those passages. The Old Testament (<u>Genesis through Malachi</u>) is foundational. In fact, we really can't fully understand or appreciate what happens in the New Testament without at least a working knowledge of what occurred in the Old Testament.

What about <u>Matthew, Mark, Luke and John</u>? These are the Gospels, written about the life and ministry of Jesus Christ. The Gospels were written so we could know and believe that Jesus is the Son of God (John 20:31). He was the example of how we should live our lives as children of God. The Gospels are also very important, but when studying these books, we need to focus on how Jesus lived and not necessarily how the disciples or other people operated. Why? Because the disciples did not have the Holy Spirit in the same way we do today. They were not filled with the Holy Spirit until after Jesus ascended and sent the Holy Spirit to earth.

<u>Acts 2-Jude</u> are the books that were written for those alive *after* Jesus' ascension to Heaven and the coming of the Holy Spirit, but *before*

the Revelation period of the anti-christ and Jesus' return. These are the books that were written in the time/era that we are living in today.

It is not that the other books of the Bible do not apply — they do. In fact, Old Testament verses are quoted by Jesus and some of the New Testament writers throughout the New Testament. However, until we understand the portion of the Bible that applies directly to us, we do not grasp how the Old Testament and some of the New Testament should be understood. We understand them *in light of* what Jesus paid for and how we walk this earth now.

This is key, so please let me repeat it one more time. Often people look at the Bible as a whole, not seeing the difference between the Old Testament, the Gospels, and time after Jesus sent the Holy Spirit. God's relationship has *not* been the same with everyone throughout history. Yes, Jesus Christ is the same yesterday, today and forever (Hebrews 13:8), but God's relationship has been different with various people and groups throughout the Bible.

From beginning to end, the Bible is written using the language of relationship and family. Using that same terminology, for example, the Bible calls Adam a son of God. Moses tells Pharaoh that Israel is God's first-born son. Jesus is the Son of God and today's believers are also called sons of God. As with any large family, Father God speaks to each son a little differently, but at the core, God's instruction has been about relationship. Now, through faith in Jesus, and by His Spirit, He has made a way for us, His "latest sons," to actually be in union with Him. Yes, you read that correctly. God made (and wanted) a way for us to be in union with Him. That is a radical and revolutionary thought, and it's true.

Do you see why it is so important to understand how portions of the Bible apply to us today? I believe the lack of understanding in this area is one of the key reasons why people think that the Bible is "confusing." They are confused because they don't understand how God's covenants impact them, and they haven't been taught to know the difference. Understanding the basic timeframes throughout Scripture helps us to understand not only what Jesus paid for, but God's Will and mission for how we must live our lives today.

To summarize, understanding who God has made us to be can only be fully appreciated through the Old *and* New Testaments. When we grasp the awesome reality of who we are in Jesus Christ, we see Old Testament Scripture from a new perspective. We see references to Jesus and what He would do for the world in many passages written hundreds of years before He was born. When we read the Old Testament, the trick is to see passages from *this side* of the cross. We see it from the finished, "now" side on the timeline, not from the anticipated, "it's coming" side.

Going forward, notice the Bible verses used in books, Bible studies, songs, sermons, and memory verses. Often they are from the Old Testament. Again, these are important to know, but often they are referring to a different relationship with God and a different set of circumstances that impacts how we apply it. This doesn't mean that we shouldn't read Old Testament books like Isaiah and Psalms, but we don't make them the primary focus (Isaiah is an AMAZING book of prophecy, by the way). The New Testament is where we need to be spending the majority of our reading and study time because that is the part of the Bible that applies to all believers living today.

ASK QUESTIONS. LOTS OF QUESTIONS

How many questions can you ask? This is the section for those with the heart of a researcher or detective. I am a question-asker (sometimes to the annoyance of Kevin) but it comes in handy when we study God's Word!

The Holy Spirit wants to give us the answers to our questions. It is His job! In this section, we give a list of questions to consider when studying the Bible. This goes along with reading a passage *in context*. The questions are: Who, What, Where, When, Why, and How.

The five "W's" and one "H" questions are considered the basics when gathering information for journalists. We apply these as we study Scripture to gain a better understanding of what was taking place. Many people never ask questions when they read the Bible. I didn't used to, but I do now!

When we ask lots of questions we force ourselves to understand more than mere words in a verse. We look at the writer, their motivation, setting, audience and more. In doing so, it's almost as if we were there ourselves! Asking these questions before starting into a book of the Bible you haven't studied is also a good exercise to gain perspective.

Below, we share a list of specific questions to unleash the detective inside you! You won't find answers to all the questions for every Scripture, and sometimes you won't feel like asking questions at all. However, looking for answers is a great way to get to know Scripture better, understand passages in context, and prepare yourself for potential questions when you share what you learned with others.

Who   Who is speaking?*
          Who was involved?
          Who was the writer?
          Who were they writing to?

*Note: The Bible records what was said, even when the person saying it was mistaken (had false beliefs). These statements are found in both Old and New Testaments. See an example in Job 1:16, where Job's servant indicates the "fire of God" burned up the sheep and servants. We know that the fire did not come from God.

(Questions continued)

What
What happened?
What was said? What did they do?
What was their motivation?
What happened before this event? After?

Where
Where did this event take place?
Where was the writer from?
Where were they when they were writing?
Where were the people for whom it was written?

When
When did the event take place?
When was it written?
When will it be fulfilled (prophecy)?

Why
Why did it happen?
Why was this written? Was it written to answer a question, share truth, deal with a problem, confront a lie, teach, or answer a question?
Why was the writer (or audience) there?
Why did those involved react like they did?

How
How did this event occur?
How did those involved feel about what happened?
How can this be applied to my life?

The above are only a few examples to help you get started. Asking these questions helps us to think through what we are reading. We don't just sit with a Bible on our lap; we engage! The more actively engaged we are during our Bible study time, the more we will get out of that time.

WHERE SHOULD I START?

What is the most important part of the Bible to read? The Bible is the inspired word of our God so ALL of it is important! All of it should be read and studied at some point. However, if you are just launching into Bible study with the tools we have given you, there are some books of the Bible that really focus on helping us understand who God made us to be through Jesus.

Jesus Christ is our Lord, and we have decided to live the rest of our lives *for* Him and *with* Him, doing what He told us to do in His Word. The Gospels and Acts 1 contain Jesus' commands and instructions to believers. The rest of the New Testament tells us who we are, what we have, and how to live our lives as believers. The New Testament begins with the life and ministry of Jesus Christ. As His disciples and ambassadors, it is crucial for us to study His life and teachings. Remember, we are reading Scripture through the lens of God's nature and character.

There is no wrong place to start, but we give our recommendations below as a guide in progression of study. The important thing is to spend time in God's Word; do not worry about how fast you seem to be progressing through the readings. Enjoy the process. This is an adventure with the Holy Spirit as our guide.

Step 1

Read Mark, James, 1 John, 2 John, 3 John, John, Ephesians, Philippians, Colossians, 1 Thessalonians, 2 Thessalonians, 1 Peter, and 2 Peter.

These books were selected with a focus on the life of Jesus as well as Paul's revelation from God about who He has made us to be (the New Man). These are some of the shorter books of the New Testament but packed with instructions for practical biblical living, with lots of encouragement and promises, too. Note: The Gospels of Matthew, Luke and Mark are similar, but we recommend Mark to start because it is the shortest. Ideally, we suggest completing step 1 twice before moving to step 2.

Step 2

Read from Matthew through Revelation

When reading Matthew, Mark, Luke, John and Acts 1, pay careful attention to what Jesus said and did (your Bible may use red text when Jesus is speaking). Slow down and focus on His words and actions. Jesus is our Lord, so what He said carries a great deal of importance.

Step 3

Read from Genesis through Malachi

Early in the Old Testament, the law was given to Moses and the Israelites and is of great significance both in the Old and New Testaments. The Old Testament is an amazing source for wisdom in living, and it is full of inspiring stories of heroes, miracles and God's faithfulness to his people.

As we read the Old Testament, we should take note of references to Jesus. There are many "types and shadows," that are symbols and *clues* as to what God had in store for mankind in the future. Also look carefully for prophecies about Jesus, appearing hundreds or thousands of years before He was born. Finally, purpose to understand the amazing benefits we have been given in the New Testament in light of the Old Testament.

It's a good idea to connect with one or more friends on a regular basis to share revelation, answered prayer and questions. It's way more fun to show-and-tell about a precious gold nugget you found with someone else. Not only does sharing biblical revelation help to plant it firmly in our minds, but it provides accountability to keep us on track and growing. Discussions, along with biblical verification, often lead to better understanding, and ultimately seeing God's truth in action in our lives! It is also a safe place to practice sharing the Bible with others.

[Kathy] Sometimes when it has been a while since I studied God's Word, I sit down with my Bible on my lap with a sinking feeling of guilt for not reading more often. I would begin with prayer apologizing to God for not doing what I should have done. I would cry and when I finally felt that I had expressed a long, truly heartfelt apology, I would begin studying the Bible. One day God interrupted my apology and showed me that He wants to spend every minute of time we have together in a growing, life-filled, loving time. Father God treasures that time and doesn't want to waste it listening to us show how sorry we are. Repentance isn't apologizing, although it can certainly contain an apology. Repentance is turning around and doing the right thing. Guilt and condemnation are not from God. If you haven't been reading the Bible, just start. God can hardly wait to reveal His Word to you.

Chapter 3: Getting the Right Mindset

Whatever we do, having the right mindset can make a big impact, and Bible study is no different. In this chapter, we ask you to step back and look at how you think. The enemy tries to put up many roadblocks, but following the simple techniques in this chapter will help you bypass several of them. My advice to you is to be honest and humble in your assessment, then attack troublesome areas with gusto! I think you'll be really glad you did. Ready? Let's go.

DO YOU REALLY BELIEVE THE BIBLE IS TRUE?

What do you believe right now? Most of us know *what* we believe, but we may not know or remember *why* we believe it. For many of us, chances are good that what we believe about the Bible came from a person or people that we trust. We saw them as a Bible expert. It may have been a pastor, a parent, an author or a friend who is involved in ministry.

Spiritual beliefs can be swayed by what is going on around us. Most of us are much more affected by outside influences than we realize. Sometimes we trust that the contents in "Christian" books, sermons, songs, movies, etc., are true simply because the tone sounds good, they use Christian words or even quote verses. It may be wonderful godly input or a deception from the enemy, but if we don't know God's Word, how can we tell? The Bible is the standard that we hold all teaching against. It is our *truth detector*.

[Kevin] I know that before I began studying the Bible systematically, I never challenged my own doctrinal beliefs. I felt that I didn't have the skills or knowledge to make those decisions, and what I believed *seemed* right — why change? At the core, I even wondered what I would do if something I had believed my whole Christian life turned out to be wrong. When I found out that I had been at least partially wrong on most things, it was very difficult. I had a choice to make. Do I believe the Bible or keep my current beliefs? Do I trust the Holy Spirit to guide me or do I only trust other people?

I am so glad I chose to believe the Bible. I think that, like me, you will be shocked to find out how many things you currently believe that are wrong. In humility, thank the Holy Spirit for showing you these areas and take joy in finding the answers!

"If what you believe (now) were not true, would you want to know it?"
Evangelist William Fay

[Kathy] One time I was asked, "Do you think we can still obtain God's promises in our lives if we have mistakes in what we believe?" My answer was a resounding "Yes!" The truth is that no one understands God's Word perfectly. No one living today has perfect doctrine. God is gracious and merciful and teaches us right where we are, BUT the closer we get to God's mindset, the more blessing, miracles, and Kingdom advancement we will see. There are huge benefits to seeing situations through God's eyes. The key is to choose to believe what the Bible says and accept God's grace as we actively and intentionally learn. I like Andrew Wommack's statement, "I haven't 'arrived,' but I've left," which means that we don't have all the answers, but we have chosen to leave our old incorrect beliefs behind.

Choose to believe the Bible

The most important decision for every person is to make Jesus the Lord and Savior of their life. We suggest that as Christians, the second most important decision is believing that the Bible is true and that Christians can understand it for themselves.

At the very foundation of our faith and Christian walk, we must first decide if we believe that the Bible is true. The question is NOT whether the Bible is true or false. The Bible is true whether we believe it or not! We make a conscious decision to believe it by trusting God; we don't have to prove every point to believe it. Only when we believe the Bible is the perfect Word of God as written in the original languages, can we begin to activate His promises in our lives by faith.

It gets better than that, though. When we choose to believe the Bible, we decide to believe that what God said about <u>us</u> is true. We choose to believe that we <u>are</u> who God says we are and that we can <u>do</u> what He says we can do. Trust me, that alone will stretch your thinking. What God has to say about who He made us to be and do is absolutely astonishing.

You cannot hope or wish that the Bible is true. You must decide to believe it — period. Trusting that our Father God will keep His promises is FAITH. The Bible is not something to "try out and see what happens," because the Word of God says we will not see God's promises fulfilled until we believe them. Have you met someone who took a verse out of the Bible and "tried it" for a while, saw nothing, and then chose not to believe that piece of Scripture based on their personal experience? "Trying it out" doesn't work. If you decide to just try it, you are hoping. According to the Bible, faith gets results; hoping does not (Romans 4:16-22).

Hoping is wishing, but believing leads to action and results.

How can I believe when I don't have all the answers? You do not have to understand every Scripture or prove every concept in order to believe the Bible. You don't need to have an answer for every critic that you meet, because <u>believing is a choice</u>. It is your personal choice that only you can make. You will be better able to answer people's questions as you mature in your faith and knowledge of the Bible.

Here's a secret to understanding the Bible: simply believe and do what it says. The truth of the Bible becomes clearer as we implement it in our lives!

Consider making a written commitment to believe the Bible in its entirety. This book contains a statement of belief, asking you to make a solemn decision to take God at His Word. Will you believe it? Will you sign it?

Before you give a quick answer, let us fully establish the commitment you are making! Here is the most difficult part: you must choose to believe it ALL. Often, people pick out some verses that they choose to believe and some they do not. The verses that are most difficult to believe are either those that include promises that are so awesome that they are almost unbelievable, or verses that we have not seen as reality yet in our lives. This is where we make a conscious decision to believe no matter what. We don't believe a verse because we have seen the results of it in this physical world; we see the results because we choose to believe. God's Word does not change. His promises are always true.

Do you believe God's Word — ALL of it? If so, carefully consider and sign the following statement of belief.

I Will Believe the Bible

- I believe that the Bible is the Word of God given to mankind.
- I believe the entire Bible as written in its original languages.
- I believe the Bible is absolutely true; it is the source of truth and is used to verify all truth.
- I believe that God divinely inspired the writers by His Holy Spirit to record exactly what God wanted us to know.
- I believe that God wants everyone to know Him so He has gave us the Bible and His Holy Spirit to help us understand it.
- I believe that I <u>can</u> read and understand the Bible.
- I will believe the Bible over: any experience that I have had, things others say/teach, or other books that I have read, because I know that feelings, experiences, and people can be wrong and I should not use them to determine truth.

Sign: _____

Date: _____

2 Timothy 3:16 — All Scripture *is* given by inspiration of God, and *is* profitable for doctrine, for reproof, for correction, for instruction in righteousness

CHALLENGE WHAT YOU BELIEVE

> [Kevin] I never really thought about challenging my beliefs or that I might be wrong on some spiritual topics. I would just read the Bible but I was not seeking truth. I liked to think that my heart and mind were open to whatever God wanted to teach me, but the truth is that I was studying the Bible, unwilling to truly challenge what I believed. I now realize I wasn't truly open because I thought everything I believed was right. I had hardened my heart toward some of God's truth. In fact, reading the Bible was pretty boring because I was reading it like an assignment my teacher gave me in school — just reading because I had to.

If we read the Bible to only support our current beliefs, then (intentionally or unintentionally) we have exalted what we believe over anything God would say. When we are open to being wrong, the Holy Spirit can show us many truths because we have not rejected what He wants to say. The Holy Spirit will not force us to do anything or go against our will. He is the Helper. He is ready and waiting for us to ask Him for help.

In this book, we discuss many techniques for Bible study, but the goal of nearly every single one is to escape our current belief system. We need to be willing to do whatever it takes to shake off the bias we have and be open to what the Holy Spirit wants to show us, even if He shows us that we have been wrong. I came to the point at which I wanted TRUTH so badly that if I had to read the Bible standing on my head to get out of my comfort zone, I'd do it!

Now when I sit down with my Bible, I have a purpose, but that purpose isn't to prove my existing belief right OR wrong. With a topic in mind, I tell God that I want to know what the Bible says about that topic. It's amazing. The Bible has opened up to me in ways I never dreamed possible. I knew I had read it from cover to cover but now I was seeing verses that I never knew existed. When I find out I have been wrong, I embrace the new truth and move forward.

Read Through the Lens of God's Nature and Character

I think that one of the biggest issues that holds people back during Bible study is having a distorted or inaccurate view of who God is and what He's like. When people sit down with God's Word they see everything in it through the lens of what they believe about God's nature and character. God's nature is who He is. For example, God is I AM (Exodus 3:14). He is eternal and omnipotent; He is a spirit. God's character is the motivation behind why He does what he does. In His Word, God tells us that He is love (1 John 4:8). We also know that He is the Healer, the Deliverer, and the Redeemer. As we read the Bible, our beliefs about God color our perception of who He is and how we interpret His motivation for everything He says through His Word.

It seems that most people think about God in one of several ways. First, people may think of God as an angry judge. They see Him as waiting and watching for people to make mistakes so He can punish them. They think He teaches believers by doing bad things to them and is just waiting for an excuse to throw people into hell.

The second group of people see God as a god of rewards, where everyone gets a trophy. They believe God will not allow anyone to go to hell. They feel they can just rest in the cradle of His care without any obligation to do anything. This view of God says that He will reward everyone and not punish anyone.

Depending on their life circumstance, some people see God as they see their earthly (human) father. This isn't a fair comparison no matter how good (or bad) an earthly father was. Our Father God, Jesus the Son and Holy Spirit cannot be compared with any human. We deceive ourselves if we try to correlate our relationship with God to any human relationship. If you have been doing that, please don't. Don't let another person be the standard by which you measure what God is like.

Another problem for some people is that they see the love of God in the same way they define human love. This makes sense because human love is what we know. For some it may mean always forgiving, to others it may be disciplining or teaching their children. Some see love as accepting every person's ideas, while others see love as affection and protection. The truth is that God's love is nothing like worldly human love. In fact, we can't even comprehend God's love without having the Holy Spirit reveal it to us.

What IS God like? Well, we would need a rather large book to do justice to that topic. To know about the nature and Character of God, we look in four places: 1. We read in the Bible what He has said about His nature and character. 2. We read about the things He has done and His will for humankind. 3. We read about Jesus, because Jesus represented God on earth. 4. We listen to the voice of the Holy Spirit.

Look at how God describes Jesus in Hebrews 1:1-3a. He says that Jesus is the "brightness of His (God's) glory and the express image of His person." Jesus perfectly represented God. In John 14:8-11 Jesus tells Philip about God (the Father) "He who has seen Me has seen the Father;" and, "The words that I speak to you I do not speak on My own authority; but the Father who dwells in Me does the works." Jesus said and did what God wanted done. To know about God, we look at Jesus.

What did Jesus do? He gave, taught, saved, healed and loved. He warned people about the consequences of sin and punishment. He fed the hungry and delivered all those who were oppressed by the devil. He told us how to live a godly life, forgave sins, and established a system so the world would hear His good news. He sacrificed Himself, destroyed the works of the devil and sent the Holy Spirit. He worked tirelessly, selflessly and never gave up. His goal was that we have life, and He gave everything so that we could have the freedom God made possible.

What is God like? I think that this is a great topic of study for everyone. We know that we were created in His image, so by knowing who He is, we also know more about who He created us to be. What does God tell us about his goals and mission for humankind? Knowing God's motivation is key!

We know that God is righteous; it is His nature. The Bible says that we are not only forgiven, but that we are righteous. In fact, we are the righteousness of God in Christ Jesus. His nature is our nature, too. When we really grasp God's nature and character, we go one step further and understand that we are in union with Him. We died to our old self and we live through Him. His nature is so much a part of who

He is that God says He *is* love. The same goes for us. We don't just love others, we *are* love. We *are* healing. We *are* life, just like Him.

What has He instructed us to do? God would never tell us to be or do something He wouldn't do Himself, which gives us great insight into what He values and thinks is important. A good list of God's character traits is found in Galatians 5:22-23a: the fruit of the Spirit.

God is the Creator, the Most High, Master, Shepherd, Healer, Protector, God with us, Judge, Prince of Peace, Redeemer, King, and Savior. God is almighty, righteous, everlasting, jealous, our provider, the victorious one, sanctifier, mighty one, our refuge, shield, fortress and deliverer. The list goes on and on. When you study the Bible, think of who God is. Set the tone of what you are reading by first thinking about God's nature and character. When we read the Bible, we don't just know *about* God, we actually *know Him*.

Note: In the paragraph above are biblical names and descriptions of God. It is an interesting and inspirational exercise to locate all the names and descriptions of our God!

How Do I Know What a Scripture Means?

How do we know what a Scripture means? There are many opinions about how to interpret the Bible. In fact, there are loads of opinions about how any form of literature should be interpreted.

Some people say that literature is like a piece of art, whose meaning is defined by the one who is viewing it. I have heard it said that the Bible means something different to every person. In fact, some believe that the Bible's meaning is subjective based on the reader, which has given rise to all sorts of controversy.

In the case of a written work like the Bible, the text should mean what the writer intended it to mean. We don't read the Bible through our imagination, we read it with the Holy Spirit. The Bible is deep, and the Holy Spirit uses the Bible to bring the truth we need, when we need it.

> "Some people read their Bibles in Hebrew, some in Greek; I like to read mine in the Holy Ghost."
> Smith Wigglesworth

I think that what people are really trying to say is that a Scripture is like a diamond, and the truths contained in that passage are like the many facets (faces) of a diamond. Depending on our vantage point, we see a different aspect of its beauty. The Bible's meaning does not change, but the facet that we see depends on what truth we are seeking, what is going on in our lives, and what the Holy Spirit brings to our attention. Some do stretch the meaning of Scripture to say all sorts of things that the Bible does not mean, but the real truths of the Bible are solid and unchanging.

Today, we have a benefit that the Bible writers did not have; we have a complete collection of what God wants to tell us through His Word. Because of this, we can glean truth across books, within the Bible's history and through the revelation of all the writers.

There is an abundance of books with advice about how to interpret Scripture, and some of them are helpful, interesting and insightful. However, the truth is that no human can stand-in as the Holy Spirit. Whether we read the Bible through our own logic and reasoning or someone else's research, it doesn't necessarily line up with biblical truth. Letting the Holy Spirit interpret Scripture takes time and practice. In this book we purposely tried to give only techniques for studying the Bible without trying to interpret if for you. We have listened to and read lots of teaching and it has been life-changing, but other people are not a substitute for studying on our own.

There are lots of resources for biblical interpretation, but in our experience, it has been the most exciting and joy-filled to simply let the Holy Spirit do His job. When we are obedient and available, He finds a way to get the answers to us. Many times He directs us to other Scriptures that help to interpret the one we are studying. Scripture interprets other Scripture. It must always agree with itself.

How Well Do You Know the Bible?

How well do you think you know the Bible? We thought we would include a little Bible quiz at this point just for fun. If you are completely new to Bible study, be encouraged to look through the questions and answers; they make great conversation starters. For the veterans, see how many you can answer correctly; the answers may surprise you!

These are not theological questions, but factoids from across the Old and New Testaments. We have targeted some trivia that is commonly misrepresented among believers. If you get them wrong, don't worry. In the past, I would have answered almost every one incorrectly until I made a hobby of collecting these sorts of questions during my Bible study time.

Take only take a few seconds to mark an answer. Please respond to every question without looking up the answers. Once you finish, check your responses using the solutions given at the end of this section. For bonus points, use the references to look up the passages and verify the answers!

Question 1: What did God strike Job with? A) Boils, B) Leprosy, C) Nothing

Question 2: How did Job's life end? A) God punished him and he died middle-aged with nothing, B) He died from old age, having twice what he initially had, C) The Bible does not clearly say.

Question 3: How many of each kind of animal did Noah take on the ark? A) 2, B) 7, C) Both

Question 4: Why was Jonah released from the belly of the fish after 3 days? A) Jonah repented and prayed, B) God told him the penalty for disobedience would be 3 days, C) We do not know

Question 5: Who threw the staff down the on the ground, where it then became a serpent? A) Moses, B) Aaron, C) Pharaoh

Question 6: In essence, what did the Lord say to Moses before the Red Sea was divided? A) Don't ask Me, you divide it, B) Do not be afraid, stand still and see your salvation, C) Both

Question 7: How was Elijah taken up to heaven? A) A fiery chariot, B) A whirlwind, C) a cloud

Question 8: Who visited Jesus in the manger in Bethlehem? A) Shepherds, B) Wise men, C) Both

Question 9: How many wise men came to visit Jesus? A) 3, B) 7, C) The Bible does not state how many

Question 10: Approximately how old was Jesus when the wise men visited him? A) 0-3 months, B) 1-2 years, C) greater than 3 years

Question 11: Did Jesus have brothers and sisters? A) Yes, B) No

Question 12: Did Jesus heal people in His hometown of Nazareth? A) Yes, B) No

Question 13: What was the woman caught in adultery doing while Jesus addressed the Scribes and Pharisees? A) Laying on the ground B) Crying, C) Standing, D) The Bible does not say

Question 14: Who was the first disciple to say "Let us also go, that we may die with Him (meaning Jesus)"? A) Doubting Thomas, B) Peter, C) One of the Sons of Thunder

Question 15: In the Gospels, besides Jesus, who else were the chief priests plotting to kill before Jesus died? A) The 12 apostles, B) Lazarus, C) No one else

Question 16: How many times was Jesus scourged at the whipping post by the Romans? A) 39, B) 40, C) The Bible does not say

Question 17: When Jesus said "My God, My God, why have You forsaken Me?" was He: A) Sharing His feelings at the time of His death, B) Quoting from the Old Testament about His death and victory, C) It does not say

Question 18: After Jesus' death, what things happened? A) The Temple veil was torn and there was an earthquake, B) Dead people appeared, C) All of the above

Question 19: How many days was Lazarus dead before Jesus raised him? A) 2, B) 3, C) 4, D) 5

Question 20: Who does Jesus consider His disciples? A) Anyone who follows His teachings, B) Everyone who was with Him when He was ministering on earth, C) Only the 12 disciples that He made apostles

How did you do? Even though this was fun, we had a strategic reason for this activity. Through our Bible study, we have noticed that some of the most basic Bible "facts" stored in our memories were actually false. These quiz questions aren't necessarily key issues for Christianity (how many wise men visited Jesus?), but it is important to know that some of the things we believe about the Bible are probably incorrect.

The main purposes of this quiz are twofold: 1. To understand how much we are influenced by movies about the Bible, post cards, commercials, etc. and 2. To show that our brains may hold some incorrect biblical "facts." A lot of these inaccuracies come from accepting wrong information from other people (who also heard it from someone with wrong information). What a bad cycle! We can only stop this cycle by verifying with the Bible ourselves. We have to believe something because it's what the Bible says, not because we saw it on television or read it on the internet.

I really want to stress the point that it is imperative to validate everything we believe with what the Bible says. Unless I have personally verified a teaching, a doctrine or a concept with Scripture, I <u>cannot</u> trust it as truth. If we believe that we already know everything about a biblical topic, then we are much less likely to see His truth; the truth on that topic can remain hidden to us. Instead, we should assume that we MAY have wrong information and be open to what God says in His Word. When we look in the Bible, we either find out we have been wrong or we find we were correct, solidify our understanding and grow. Regardless, we win.

Answer 1: C) Nothing — Job 2:7

Answer 2: B) Old age having twice what he initially had — Job 1:3-Job 42:12-17

Answer 3: C) 7 clean and 2 unclean — Genesis 7:1-3

Answer 4: A) Jonah repented and prayed — Jonah 2:1-10

Answer 5: B) Aaron — Exodus 7:10

Answer 6: A) Do not ask me, you divide it — Exodus 14:13-16

Answer 7: B) Whirlwind — 2 Kings 2:10-11

Answer 8: A) Shepherds — Luke 2:8-20, Matthew 2:11 (the wise men went to His house)

Answer 9: C) It does not say — Luke 2:7-16, Matthew 2:1-11

Answer 10: B) 1-2 years — Matthew 2:16

Answer 11: A) Yes — Mark 3:31-32, Mark 6:3, Matt 13:55

Answer 12: A) Yes — Mark 6:5

Answer 13: C) Standing — John 8:3-11 (9)

Answer 14: A) (Doubting) Thomas — John 11:16

Answer 15: B) Lazarus — John 12:9-10

Answer 16: C) It does not say — Matthew 27:26, Mark 15:15, John 19:1, 2 Corinthians 11:24 (where the belief of 39 may have come from)

Answer 17: B) Quoting the Old Testament about His death and victory — Matt 27:46, Psalm 22

Answer 18: C) All of the above — Matt 27:51-53

Answer 19: C) 4 — John 11:39

Answer 20: A) Anyone who follows His teachings — John 8:31, Matthew 10:2 & Luke 6:13 (12 apostles)

Chapter 4: Relying on Him

The Bible's meaning explodes when we read it with the Holy Spirit's help and revelation. It takes time and practice, but learning to study God's Word with the one who inspired the words within is worth the effort. It's priceless.

Prayer is Key

In the following chapters, we go into practical ways to get truth out of God's Word. To start, this may seem obvious, but many people overlook the massive benefit of praying before and after Bible study. Things you may want to pray for are revelation, insight, and understanding on what you are about to read. Tell Him that you want to know the truth and ask Him to make it clear to you.

For example, if you are trying to find truth about Christ in you and how you are a new creation, then focus on that very thought when you pray. In your mind and heart, ask, "Who am I in Jesus? What does it mean to be a new creation?" Now just sit and be quiet for a bit. Make time for God to speak to you. Sit in a quiet place. Think of it as a real conversation where you ask God a question and then wait for an answer. Treat Him with the respect that you would give another person and know the He always hears and He always answers. Hearing His voice takes practice.

At this point, God may give you somewhere to start in your study, and words may come into your head related to that topic, or even pictures. You may get a thought in your mind that you know didn't come from you. Sometimes, you just know when it's Him. God communicates with each of us differently.

He may guide you into a new area to search out. Make certain to have a notebook and a pen or two with you! Write everything down. Don't worry if you do not hear anything new from God as you pray; simply go ahead and begin studying the topic that is on your mind. Remember that He knows what we need to learn better than we do *and* He knows what is holding us back. Jump in and trust Him.

After Bible study, thank Father God for the revelation that He gave or will give you. Allow the Holy Spirit some time to answer your questions. Thank Him for helping you to understand. If you don't understand at first, don't get frustrated, and don't give up! Keep praying for understanding and truth. It will come.

> [Kathy] I have heard people refer to their time with God as a "quiet time." There are many benefits to having quiet time with God, but my house is rarely quiet. In fact, it is a wonderfully noisy place! In different seasons of life we will have more or less "quiet time" with God. If we are obedient and dedicated to spending time in the Bible and prayer, He is faithful to reveal truth and answer our questions no matter how *quiet* our time is. He can get through to us whether we are driving or making supper. We take advantage of that precious time with Him and He is faithful. The Holy Spirit is truly wonderful at His job!

Revelation from the Holy Spirit is Awesome

Have you ever read a passage many times through the years, and then one day something just "clicked," and you received an exciting new "revelation" of truth? This revelation came from God Himself through His Word directly to you. Revelation from the Bible through the Holy Spirit is what opens our eyes to truth and helps us to renew our minds so that we can make God's promises come alive. And it doesn't stop there. We begin to think the way God thinks, understand who He is and who He has made us to be. If you have never experienced receiving God's revelation in Scripture, get ready, because you will!

> [Kevin] One day when I was reading, I got one of the biggest revelations that I have ever received. I quickly found Kathy and told her, "The God who created the entire universe, lives in ME!" Kathy was working on the computer, nodded her head and agreed. I said, "No, you don't understand, the GOD WHO CREATED THE ENTIRE UNIVERSE, LIVES IN ME!!!" Kathy agreed and said, "I already knew that Kevin." But she wasn't really appreciating the significance of what God showed me.
>
> About one week later Kathy was sitting in the living room and that same revelation hit her, too. At first Kathy said it quietly. "Kevin, God really lives in us." Then she said it much louder. "Kevin, GOD really lives in US! That's AMAZING!" I got excited because we could finally really talk about this wonderful fact. This is what Christianity is all about — Christ in YOU!

It is one thing to know a fact in our head, but it is totally different when the Holy Spirit reveals it to us. <u>Knowledge is NOT revelation</u>. Revelation is WAY BETTER. As our friend, Stephanie Blake says, "You've got to know it in your knower." Revelation is when that Biblical truth that you know as a fact suddenly comes to life. It's almost as if that truth moves from your mind to your heart. It goes from a fact to a reality.

Think back to math class in school. It was one thing to see the teacher work a math problem on the board, and quite another when the math concept really "clicked." It is like a light bulb turns on in our mind and we just "get it." That's how revelation feels. Scripture we have seen many times suddenly comes to life with meaning. Revelation doesn't have to be deep and profound, but it is always full of meaning, no matter how simple it is. One of the most impacting revelations I have ever received is that God loves me.

Part of the reason that Jesus left and went to Heaven was so that He could send back the Holy Spirit to live inside of every believer. Once Jesus became human, He could not physically teach each person on earth. This is why Jesus said in John 16:7 that **it was better for us that He went**, because then the Holy Spirit would be sent to us.

God's Ways May Not Seem Logical

As we read the Bible, we realize that God's way of thinking is often completely opposite of human logic. For example, people say, "I'll believe it when I see it," but God says, "You'll see it when you believe it." We shouldn't be surprised when we find statements in the Bible that don't agree with worldly logic. The enemy would like nothing better than for people to think that God's ways are ridiculous by promoting his deception of worldly logic which is often the exact opposite of godly wisdom.

> **Proverbs 16:25** — There is a way that seems right to a man, but its end is the way of death.

If a Scripture does not make sense at first, we shouldn't apply our human logic and guess at an answer. Technically, it is not our job to figure it out. Our job is to believe it; the Holy Spirit's job is to bring God's Word to life. I have found that the fastest way to understand is to expectantly rest in knowing that the Holy Spirit is working to get me the answer, like a child waiting to open a gift.

I Have the Mind of Christ?

The Holy Spirit is to us now as Jesus was to His earthly disciples: He is our Teacher, Comforter and Revealer of Truth. He is our connection to the Father. One of the Holy Spirit's primary jobs is to reveal truth in the Bible as we study.

> **1 Corinthians 2:16** — For "who has known the mind of the Lord that he may instruct Him?" But <u>we have the mind of Christ</u>.

Having the mind of Christ (Holy Spirit) operating in us is to have Christ's thoughts, plans and wisdom inside of us. In the natural, we do not think God's thoughts, but with the Holy Spirit, we can! The wisdom and knowledge of God are always working inside of us, but it is up to us to listen and obey it. The more we start thinking in line with Him and are open to truth, the more *automatic* this process becomes.

1 John 2:20 — But <u>you have an anointing</u> from the Holy One, and <u>you know all things</u>.

In 1 John 2:20 we see that God sent us the anointing, which *is* the Holy Spirit. Take a minute to think about this. As a believer, you have the Holy Spirit, so you have access to the mysteries of God. As a believer, the Spirit of God inside us knows all things even though our natural human mind does not.

John 14:16-17 — [16] And I will pray the Father, and He will give you another Helper, that He may abide with you forever— [17] <u>the Spirit of truth</u>, whom the world cannot receive, because it neither sees Him nor knows Him; but you know Him, <u>for He dwells with you and will be in you</u>.

In John 14:17, Jesus describes the Holy Spirit as the "Spirit of Truth." His job is to lead us into <u>all truth</u>! The Holy Spirit reveals the wisdom and knowledge of God, and also serves as a *truth detector* on spiritual and physical things. The Holy Spirit will show us truth from lies, and most of the time He does this through the Bible.

The Holy Spirit *can* give us revelation on a concept or Scripture we have never seen or heard before. However, this has not been our experience. Most of the time He uses Scripture we already know to answer our questions. Like pieces of a puzzle, the Holy Spirit uses Scriptures to teach us a concept. This is why studying and memorizing Scripture is so important! The more Bible that we know, the easier it is for the Holy Spirit to get answers to us.

Key to getting revelation

> [Kathy] Get desperate. For me, it is the times when I am truly desperate to know something from God that I get revelation on it more quickly and in more quantity (Matthew 7:7). Some call it perseverance, and some may call it stubbornness, but when I set my mind on getting God's answer to a question, I keep asking and knocking until I get an answer. Getting an answer can consume my thoughts. I will even excitedly point to my notebook and tell God, "I'm waiting for an answer to my question, and I'm ready to write it down!" It is this attitude of expectation and persistence that can help speed the answers to us. I believe that God answers right away, but we sometimes have difficulty hearing the answer due to our own thoughts or the enemy's interference. But God keeps on working to get us the answer. God never gives up and neither should we.

Often my biggest revelations come when I am doing ordinary, everyday tasks. Sometimes it is when I'm getting ready in the morning or lying in bed ready to sleep. Sometimes revelation comes when I'm driving my kids to events or when I'm cleaning the house. Just because I don't receive revelation while I'm studying the Bible doesn't mean that I missed it. God knows how to get through to us if we give Him a chance and listen.

> [Kevin] For me, it seems like my biggest revelations generally happen during or right after prayer, listening to the Bible while driving, or when I am awakened early in the morning. I try to quickly write it down and then search the Bible. It seems like the process of searching the Bible after receiving the revelation really cements it into my mind.

Important Note on Revelation

It is important to note that the personal revelation we get from the Holy Spirit will NEVER contradict the Bible. Many people have been led away from the truth by getting so-called, "new revelation." They thought it was new truth from God's angels, the Holy Spirit, or Jesus Christ Himself, but in fact is was a deception from Satan. We were warned about this in 2 Peter and 2 Corinthians. ALL revelation must be verified and agree completely with the Bible. God's revelation to us will always line up with the Bible.

> **2 Peter 1:19-2:1** — [19] And so we have the prophetic word confirmed, which you do well to heed as a light that shines in a dark place, until the day dawns and the morning star rises in your hearts; [20] knowing this first, <u>that no prophecy of Scripture is of any private interpretation</u>, [21] for prophecy never came by the will of man, but holy men of God spoke as they were moved by the Holy Spirit.
> [1] But <u>there were also false prophets among the people, even as there will be false teachers among you, who will secretly bring in destructive heresies</u>, even denying the Lord who bought them, *and* bring on themselves swift destruction.

> **2 Cor 11:13-15** — [13] For such *are* <u>false apostles, deceitful workers, transforming themselves into apostles of Christ</u>. [14] And no wonder! For <u>Satan himself transforms himself into an angel of light</u>. [15] Therefore it is no great thing if his ministers also transform themselves into ministers of righteousness, whose end will be according to their works.

Satan wants to destroy the Church and rob it of power through lack of knowledge and false beliefs. He tries to destroy the church from the outside AND the inside. I was shocked when I did a word search* on the word *false* in the New Testament. The resulting verses revealed some strategies of the enemy that you may find astonishing.

> **Hosea 4:6** — My people are destroyed for lack of knowledge.

*We cover word searches in more detail in the section, "Key Word Searches."

Keep It Simple.
Stop Searching for Hidden Meanings

In an effort to get deep understanding and truth, people often look for hidden meanings in Scripture. They try to read between the lines to see the *hidden* truth because they think that's what it takes to get revelation out of the Bible. Let's start this section by saying that God can speak to us multitudes of ways but the Bible is not about conjuring up ideas and connecting dots that were never meant to be connected.

Don't get me wrong — God is deep. No one besides the Spirit of God has ever come to the end of the knowledge and wisdom God has to share through His Word. We could study all day, every day for the rest of our lives and never get to the end, and that's great! The more I learn from the Bible, the more I realize that everything He teaches me is simple. It's so simple, in fact, that I don't understand why I never saw it before. This is where we see God's true genius. His concepts are life-altering, earth-shaking and simple at the same time. Truly brilliant.

If you can't explain it simply, you don't understand it well enough.
Albert Einstein

One of the most common places people look for secret hidden meaning are in the parables. Jesus' parables are sometimes expanded and analyzed to bring out points that were never intended. Bob Spurlock, our good friend and a Messianic believer, shared with us the history and first-century custom of Jewish parables. A parable is an illustration, or a story told to share a single truth; the story's intent was to help us remember that truth. Jesus' parables were not simple or simplistic. They are often very deep, but there is rarely more than one point being made.

When we read the parables that Jesus told, we are not supposed to read into every detail and extract a hidden symbolic insight behind every detail. The customary goal of a parable was to share a story to remember a point. For example, consider Jesus' parable about the rich man, the camel and the eye of the needle (Matthew 19:24). The point is not to spiritualize how a rich man is like a camel, or how he has to be unburdened (no camels were permitted in Jewish city walls). It is simply to illustrate that many things seem <u>impossible</u>. BUT, even though it may seem impossible to man, with God, all things are possible.

Following are portions of two parables Jesus told. Pay special attention to what Jesus said right *before* He told the parable.

> **Luke 18:1-5** — ¹ Then He spoke a parable to them, that men <u>always ought to pray and not lose heart</u>, ² saying: "There was in a certain city a judge who did not fear God nor regard man. ³ Now there was a widow in that city; and she came to him, saying, 'Get justice for me from my adversary.' ⁴ And he would not for a while; but afterward he said within himself, 'Though I do not fear God nor regard man, ⁵ yet because this widow troubles me I will avenge her, lest by her continual coming she weary me.'"

What is the main point of this parable from Luke 18? Jesus tells us in verse one, "that men always ought to pray and not lose heart." He was saying, "Keep going; don't give up until you have the victory!"

> **Luke 19:11-13** — ¹¹ Now as they heard these things, He spoke another parable, because He was near Jerusalem and <u>because they thought the kingdom of God would appear immediately</u>. ¹² Therefore He said: "A certain nobleman went into a far country to receive for himself a kingdom and to return. ¹³ So he called ten of his servants, delivered to them ten minas, and said to them, 'Do business till I come.'

In Luke 19 we can see in verse 11 why Jesus was telling them the parable. He was essentially saying, "I will be gone for a time. Until I return, keep doing what you were commanded until I return and you will be rewarded according to your accomplishments." In these two parables, it says what the point of the parable is. We don't have to guess.

Why do people say that God's Word is mysterious? Well, God said that He kept Jesus' mission a mystery for a long time so that the enemy could not foil His plan. God's plan was Jesus coming to earth to die as a sacrifice for our sins, defeat the enemy, ascend to Heaven and send the Holy Spirit to all believers.

Colossians 1:25-27 — ²⁵of which I became a minister according to the stewardship from God which was given to me for you, to fulfill the word of God, ²⁶ the <u>mystery</u> which has been hidden from ages and from generations, but now <u>has been revealed</u> to His saints. ²⁷ To them <u>God willed to make known</u> what are the riches of the glory <u>of this mystery among the Gentiles: which is Christ in you, the hope of glory</u>.

His mystery is *Christ in YOU, the hope of glory*. That's it! He isn't hiding anything anymore. In fact, He has sent the Holy Spirit to lead us into all truth! He has given us His Word and the Teacher!

Mark 10:15 — Assuredly, I say to you, whoever does not <u>receive the kingdom of God as a little child</u> will by no means enter it.

God wants us to receive His Kingdom as a little child. Whatever their parents say, children believe as truth, and then act accordingly. Children don't look for secret hidden meanings. When a parent says to their young child, "If you clean your room I will give you a cookie," the child runs to clean up their room. They trust that they will get the cookie promised to them if they are obedient.

2 Corinthians 11:3 — But I fear, lest somehow, as the serpent deceived Eve by his craftiness, so your minds may be corrupted from <u>the simplicity that is in Christ</u>.

God says that in Christ is simplicity. Jesus' message is simple, and our Father God designed the Bible to be simple. The devil is the one who works to complicate and corrupt it! If the devil can confuse us and muddle our thinking, we won't know what to believe. He wants to get us to doubt and waver in our belief.

If you are working hard to find hidden meanings and messages inside the Bible, stop. Simply believe what the passage says, and ask the Holy Spirit to give you revelation on that verse. Here is a secret to getting deep biblical understanding: choose to believe the Bible and do what it says to do. When we see it work, we reach an entirely new level of understanding. If we believe that the Bible is difficult to understand, it will be. If we think the Bible is easy to understand, things become clearer.

Here's an inspiring quote from John Alexander Dowie as taken from *God's Generals* by Roberts Liardon. Dowie is facing an epidemic that is killing his parishioners and countless others in his town. Notice the revelation Dowie receives from God.

> "And there I sat with sorrow-bowed head for my afflicted people, until the bitter tears came to relieve my burning heart. Then I prayed for some message… Then the words of the Holy Ghost inspired in Acts 10:38 stood before me all radiant with light, revealing Satan as the Defiler, and Christ as the Healer. My tears were wiped away, my heart was strong, I saw the way of healing…I said, 'God help me now to preach the Word to all the dying around, and tell them how 'tis Satan still defiles, and Jesus still delivers, for He is just the same today.'…in a strange way it came to pass…the sword I needed was still in my hands…and never will I lay it down. The doctor, a good Christian man, was quietly walking up and down the room… Presently, he stood at my side and said, 'Sir, are not God's ways mysterious?' 'God's way!...No sir, that is the devil's work and it is time we called on Him Who came to "destroy the work of the devil"'
>
> John Alexander Dowie

Are you wondering how the story ends? The doctor left the room. Dowie boldly prays and sees not just that one healing, but numerous miraculous healings following this revelation from God. From that point, no more of his parishioners died from the epidemic.

DON'T ADD REQUIREMENTS

We need to understand that God gave us everything we need to get started in the Bible. It is vital to know that God's promises apply to us today, and He wants us to live with His promises active in our lives all the time. Many people say they believe the promises in the Bible, but when it comes right down to it, they don't believe the promises are available the way the Bible says they are. Many think there are additional exceptions and stipulations to receive what God has for them.

> **Matthew 21:21** — So Jesus answered and said to them, "Assuredly, I say to you, <u>if you have faith and do not doubt</u>, you will not only do what was done to the fig tree, but also if you say to this mountain, 'Be removed and be cast into the sea,' it will be done."

What were Jesus' requirements? 1. Have faith and 2. Don't doubt. However, when we talk to people we hear lots of additional requirements that Jesus never said. Have you heard any of these?

I will receive God's promise if:

- It is God's timing
- I have enough faith and the right kind of faith
- I don't have un-repented sin in my life
- There are no generational curses
- There is an open heaven
- The anointing is here
- I have not opened a door to the devil
- It is according to God's mysterious plan

Where do these additional requirements come from? It is usually a response to unanswered prayer. When we have prayed and do not get the desired result, we look for reasons why. Those *reasons* are often deceptions from the enemy that people believe as "new truth" from God. Perhaps someone at church received what they were believing for after they spent a long time repenting, or they went through a process of eliminating "roadblocks to unanswered prayer." After the word got out, others followed the same process and some saw results.

This does not mean that there are additional requirements established by God. Matthew 21:21 still says 1. Have faith and 2. Don't doubt.

There is a lot of power in faith. If a person is believing God will answer their prayer if they perform additional steps, then they are placing their faith in those steps. Due to the faith they are placing in those steps, they may see their prayers answered. This doesn't mean that God has these requirements, but the people aren't allowing themselves to have faith in God until after they have followed the additional steps. To know what the requirements are for every one of God's promises, we look at:

1. What does the Bible say (or not say)?
2. What did Jesus say and do?

When we put additional requirements on receiving God's promises, we take a promise that we can receive simply and easily by grace (a sure thing!) and demote it to a complicated game of guessing whether we have met all the criteria. When we are guessing and hoping, we can't have faith. The enemy delights in getting people to add conditions to receiving what Jesus has already paid for. We allow the enemy to spin us around and around like a dog chasing its tail, trying to figure out what more needs to be done until we eventually give up. This is precisely what these additional requirements do. The enemy is crafty. Reject his deceptions. Know the covenant (contract). Know what is yours.

God does not lie, and He does not exaggerate. God means what He says. We do not add or subtract! We are to live out the truth that He gave us in His Word just the way He said to do it.

STOP READING COMMENTARIES

What is a biblical commentary? Usually a Bible commentary appears at the bottom of each page below the Scripture. In the commentary, a person has written their own interpretation of what a piece of Scripture means. They may also attempt to give insight into the culture of that time period or discuss how to apply a principle in life. The word *commentary* simply means comments, explanations or opinions.

What is most important to know is that a Bible commentary is not Scripture. It is someone's belief about what each passage means. Many read commentary because they think that they cannot understand what the Bible says on their own. Sometimes people have been told that they cannot interpret Scripture without "proper training," or perhaps they heard a teaching about how a passage has a hidden meaning and doesn't really mean what it says.

The enemy would be happy to convince people that they cannot understand their Bible, placing an invisible barrier between them and the truth. We know that God's Word is the sword of the Spirit. Through deception the enemy disarms believers by keeping them from knowing and applying God's Word.

If you are someone who feels the constant need to read biblical commentary, purchase a Bible that doesn't have any.

When we read someone else's opinion about the meaning of a passage, it can be more challenging to receive revelation from the Holy Spirit. Our mind becomes biased toward what was said in the commentary. If the commentary writer had difficulty believing God's promise in a Scripture, then they may state that it is figurative, not intended for today, or insert other requirements that God never said.

Is commentary ever good? Yes! Sometimes commentary includes fascinating tidbits about historical placement and cultural effects of the time the Scripture was written. However, even though some types of commentary can be helpful and may contain amazing insight into Scripture, it is not the same as getting revelation directly from the Holy Spirit. True, abiding, life-changing revelation does not usually come from listening to other people; we must get it for ourselves.

When we are starting into Bible study, it is best to strip away human input and trust what will be revealed by the Holy Spirit through the

Word of God to you. Commentary will make it more difficult to be unbiased during study. At the heart, we need to care about what God says, not people!

Another sneaky form of commentary

Many Bibles display headings above certain portions of Scripture to help the reader locate topics. Use caution, as these headings can also be a form of commentary leading toward certain beliefs. Some translations may include a heading like this: *Jesus Breaks the Sabbath*. We know that this is not true. What Jesus broke were the traditions of man, not the laws that God established.

We have heard people say, "Through my study of the Bible I just found out that a key doctrine I have believed my whole life is wrong!" You are not alone! There is not a single person that has reached a full understanding of the Bible. Not one alive today. But that's not a good reason to keep beliefs that are unbiblical. We must be dedicated to seeking, believing, and putting God's truth into practice no matter what. Use what you know, but always aim to know the Bible (and its author) more.

Chapter 5: Getting to Know Your Bible

It was only a few years ago that we began to understand the importance of knowing the basics of how the Bible was translated and what people have added to the original text. It helped us gain perspective as well as prepare us for deeper study in the original writings.

READ A GOOD TRANSLATION

Unless we can read the Old Testament in Hebrew/Chaldean and the New Testament in Greek, we are not reading the Bible how it was written initially. The Bible has been translated into a language we understand. There are numerous translations of the Bible, but not all are equally accurate. Here is an example of differences in translation from John 3:16.

John 3:16 (Easy-to-Read ERV) Yes, God loved the world so much that he gave his only Son, so that everyone who believes in him would not be lost but have eternal life.

John 3:16 (New King James NKJV) For God so loved the world that He gave His only begotten Son, that whoever believes in Him should not perish but have everlasting life.

The difference between the ERV and NKJV translations is subtle, but important. We know that if we don't accept God's free gift of salvation by receiving Jesus Christ as our Lord and Savior, we will spend eternity in hell. The word *perish* in the NKJV is much more devastating than simply being *lost* in the ERV. When we look deeper into the meaning of the biblical Greek word, we see that the word *perish* seems to provide a meaning closer to the author's intent. There will be more on how to study biblical Greek later

In this chapter, we discuss why certain translations can be less reliable, and then list our top recommendations for Bible study.

Translating from Greek or Hebrew to English is Imprecise

Creating a new translation of the Bible has been a very difficult task. Each language has particular quirks or constructs that are specific to the people who speak it. Some words and phrases used by the writers of the Bible literally have no exact word-for-word translation into another language. The translator had to find a way to relay the same ideas using a totally different set of words, language, and culture.

Translators may introduce bias

Bible translations come from translators who are human beings, each with their own spiritual beliefs and doctrinal biases. To translate, a person must first interpret what it means in the original, and then translate that meaning into the new language. It is naïve to think that any person could successfully translate the Scriptures without injecting even a hint of their own bias or beliefs.

In some cases, a Bible translation may have been written using modern phrases and words to make it more relevant to today's culture. The outcome may be easier to understand initially but might result in a watered-down Bible that loses some of the power of God's promises.

Translations may contain errors

In our study of other translations, we were initially excited about a few of them until we noticed how some of the promises in the Bible were diluted into mere suggestions. The impact and assurance of the statements was removed. We saw Scriptures that were mistranslated and words or entire verses that were added or changed. More and more Bible translations are coming out today to align with modern trends and political correctness. The only thing that matters is God's truth, and we must select a translation that is as true to the original as possible.

Don't get me wrong; we are profoundly thankful for the devoted people who spent years translating the Bible. Entire teams of scholars have dedicated their lives to analyzing manuscripts to give us the closest version of the Bible in our language. What a gift of labor and love to humankind! Overall, the translators of many mainstream versions have done a remarkable job.

We simply need to realize that there can be slight imperfections both in how words were translated and in how we interpret the words they selected. The variations in translations are usually very minimal. When we appreciate translations for what they are, we understand that we should never make an entire doctrine out of a single word or phrase. Later in this book you will learn how to analyze verses in their written language, which allows us to get even closer to the original writer's intent.

The truth is that there is no perfect translation, but there are some that are more accurate and reliable overall. Each translation has strengths and weaknesses. There are some translations that seem to really capture the original intent in one passage but are lacking in other passages. In our search for the most accurate translations, we considered not only our own experience but the experience of some with many more years of study. We have no doubt that there are other good translations out there, but we have not reviewed them yet.

There are two basic types of Bible translations: Formal Equivalence (FE) and Dynamic Equivalence (DE). The main difference is that FE versions have been created by substituting an equivalent word or phrase from the original Greek or Hebrew word or phrase, and DE paraphrases or substitutes an equivalent thought. We summarize this by saying FE are *word-for-word* translations and DE are *thought-for-thought* translations. There are even some translations that combine the FE and DE methods to produce a hybrid. Translations we have recommended for primary study fall in the FE category, and those for companion study belong primarily in the DE category. It is good to be aware of what type we are reading, and to know that both types are powerful when used for their strengths.

Following are some of the translations that we recommend based on our review. Before purchasing, look through several at the local Christian bookstore or read online. Each list is given in order of our perceived readability, from easiest to more difficult. When you are ready for a challenge, look at the Dake Annotated Reference Bible. While it may not be the easiest to read at first, it contains an abundance of cross references.

Primary Study translations (word-for-word)
- Young's Literal Translation of the Bible (YLT)
- New King James Version (NKJV)
- New American Standard (NAS or NASB)
- King James Version (KJV)
- The Dake Annotated Reference Bible (KJV)

Companion translations (thought-for-thought)

The following are good companions for Bible study, but we do not recommend them as primary study Bibles. Both of these enrich study by expanding the meaning to try to bring across the original writer's intent.

The Amplified Bible (AMP)

Many have found the Amplified Bible to be very helpful in expanding, or *amplifying* the meaning of certain words with the goal of bringing across the original writer's intent.

The New Testament: An Expanded Translation (WET)
By Kenneth Wuest

We commonly refer to this book as the *Wuest Bible*. The Wuest Bible is quite different than most versions. Instead of a word-for-word translation, Wuest paraphrases the New Testament meaning-for-meaning or thought-for-thought. It could be considered more of an *interpretation* than a *translation*. The Wuest Bible is intended to relay how a first century Greek person would understand each passage, using as many words as needed to convey the meaning. The *Wuest New*

Appreciate Your Bible's Notation

Reading through your Bible, have you noticed little superscripted letters and numbers? Have you noticed italicized words? There is a whole system of notation that goes into some Bibles, and each type helps the reader in a different way.

Example

Romans 8:1 — *There is* therefore now no condemnation to those who are in Christ Jesus,[a] who do not walk according to the flesh, but according to the Spirit [1].

In this example, we see that, *There is*, is italicized and notice the superscripted [a] after *Christ Jesus* and a *1* after Spirit. These are some examples of biblical notation.

Take some time to read the notes in your Bible* that explain what various notations mean such as cross references, special fonts, letters, numerals, symbols and even colors. As special notations come up in your study, learn what each stands for. It is worth the time. In this chapter we cover only some of the most common types of notation. Some study Bibles have notation that is not explained in this book.

*An index of what various types of notation mean is commonly found in the front.

Italics

In some translations, you will likely find italicized words (slightly slanted text that looks like this: *italicized*). These italicized words were not translated from the biblical Greek or Hebrew manuscripts, but were added by translators to help the reader understand the Scripture. When translating from one language to another, they considered it necessary to add words to convey the meaning of the passage. Remember that these words were added to help us understand the passage as the *translator* understood it.

Depending on the verse, these added italicized words may accurately bring more understanding or could introduce error. It is possible for an added word to significantly change the meaning of a sentence, and that meaning may not be consistent with the meaning of the original writer and God. For this reason, it's a good idea to get a Bible that uses notation to show those words that have been added by the translators.

Note: It is a good practice to read a passage <u>with</u> and <u>without</u> the italicized words. In some cases, the meaning changes substantially when they are removed.

Here's an example. In 1 Corinthians 12 is the passage that talks about the ministry and manifestation of the Holy Spirit in the lives of believers.

1 Corinthians 12:1 — Now concerning spiritual *gifts*, brethren, I do not want you to be ignorant:

In 1 Corinthians 12:1 we see that the word, *gifts* is italicized. This means that the word *gifts* was added by the translators. Read the verse without the word *gifts*. When we step back and think about what this passage means without the word, *gifts*, Paul is saying that he does not want the Corinthians to be ignorant about spiritual matters. Then he goes on to talk about how the Spirit works in and through disciples of Jesus Christ. In the Young's Literal Translation it says, "And concerning the spiritual things…" *Things* is quite different from *gifts*. For this reason, we recommend utilizing multiple translations when studying Scripture.

In school when we learn to write a paper, we usually indicate what the entire paper will be about in the first sentence or two. People looking at 1 Corinthians 12 may read verse 1 and their mindset/expectation is gifts, so they assume that the entire section is talking about spiritual gifts. How does this change our understanding? Read the verses 1-11, and in verse 1, instead of *spiritual gifts*, use the phrase *spiritual matters*. I encourage you to read the entire passage again and see this passage with new eyes, noticing all the italicized words and absorbing how the meaning would change if those words were not there.

Scripture designated as NU text

The Bible we have today was not based on a single manuscript. There are literally thousands of ancient biblical manuscripts that have been found. Many Bible books and book fragments have been found spanning thousands of years because they were copied over and over by hand through time. Given the timespan and number of people who produced copies, it is remarkable how precisely the text was copied. In the cases where the manuscripts vary, the documents have been compared against each other, taking into consideration where they were found, when they were written, and how accurate they are thought to be. Many scholars and experts then compiled what we know as the Bible today.

There is still debate among scholars about which verses should be included the Bible and those which should not. Some Bibles have special notation, such as superscripted characters, to show which passages are in question. Here is an example from Matthew 17:15-21. In this passage the disciples have just failed to heal an epileptic boy. Some Bibles may leave the verse out entirely, or they may contain a footnote as shown below: [a]. Some Bibles include verse 21 without any notation.

> **Matthew 17:20-21** — [20] ...if you have faith as a mustard seed, you will say to this mountain, 'Move from here to there,' and it will move; and nothing will be impossible for you. [21] However, this kind does not go out except by prayer and fasting. [a]

Footnotes: a. Matthew 17:21 NU-Text omits this verse.

The superscripted [a] at the end of verse 21 shows us that additional information about that verse is located under the *a* footnote on the page. In this case, the footnote is telling us that the Nestle-Aland Greek New Testament (N) and in the United Bible Societies' fourth edition (U) do not include verse 21. The NU text is based on the oldest manuscripts of the Bible, but not the most numerous manuscripts. Essentially, this means that some scholars feel this verse is a legitimate portion of original Scripture and others do not. Thousands of biblical manuscripts have been found throughout history, and scholars and historical experts must decipher which are the oldest and most accurate. Even though there are thousands of documents, it is amazing how consistent the Bible is throughout.

Before we discuss the validity of Matthew 17:21, let's address one of the foundational principles for studying the Bible: Scripture verifies itself. However, as we said in the section on translations, slight inconsistencies have appeared. When we see a verse we are not quite sure about, we check it against other Scriptures. Scripture must always agree with Scripture. We have chosen to believe that the Bible is God's Word, so we have accepted that the Bible is true. Since we agree that it is true, we understand the meaning of Scriptures that are unclear by checking them against Scripture that *is* clear.

Through our study of Matthew 17:21, we believe this verse was added later and is not divinely inspired for several reasons. First, when Jesus told the disciples why the epileptic boy in this passage did not get healed He said it was "because of your (disciples) unbelief." If Matthew 17:21 is valid, then it does not make sense that Jesus would have identified unbelief as the cause, told them nothing would be impossible if they commanded in faith, and then finished by telling them that prayer and fasting were necessary to cast it out.

Let's check this Scripture by verifying it with other Scripture. If fasting and prayer were truly necessary to cast out demons, then Jesus would have instructed the disciples to pray and fast before He send them out. We know from a passage in Mark that Jesus was questioned as to why His disciples did not fast (Mark 2:18-20), and Jesus replied that while He was with them, they would not fast. If fasting was required to cast out the demon from the epileptic boy, then Jesus would have instructed them to fast.

It is possible that Matthew 17:21 is a verse that was added by someone later to try to help people to cast out devils based on their personal belief or experience. Others believe that this verse should be included, but that Jesus was not referring to the *kind* of demon, but rather the *kind* of unbelief that needed to go out. In other words, they believe that Jesus was telling the disciples how to rid themselves of their unbelief in verse 21.

We encourage you to study this passage and others that have the *NU-Text omits* markings to see what God shows you. We include examples in this book from our own study to give you ideas about how these principles may be applied, but you should never accept any teaching about the Bible without verification — even ours!

Cross references

Cross references are a powerful tool and amazing time-saver. Cross references are simply references from one area of Scripture to another that contains information on the same topic. Sometimes when I want to drill down on a topic, I go from cross reference to cross reference until I'm satisfied that I have a grasp of that subject. They are usually noted in Scripture with superscripted characters and the corresponding information is often shown in the margin (toward the edge of the page).

As we stated before, Scripture verifies and interprets itself. If we are ever unclear about a passage, finding a cross reference to another Scripture can provide clarity. Even when I understand a verse, I feel compelled to look at the cross references as if I'm looking for buried treasure. It would be nearly impossible for Bibles to list all cross references in the margins, but an exhaustive list can be found in a reference such as *The Treasury of Scripture Knowledge* by R.A. Torrey and John Canne. We include this wonderful resource later in our list of recommendations.

THE SECRET ABOUT CHAPTER, VERSE, AND PUNCTUATION

The Bible that we have today has some additional conventions that were not present in the original manuscripts such as chapter and verse separators, and punctuation such as commas and periods. Again, this can change the meaning of Scripture, so to understand clearly we must take these things into consideration.

Don't get me wrong, chapter and verse separators are great tools to help us quickly locate a Scripture. However, they can also incorrectly break up the author's thought and alter the meaning of a passage. Ideas that should have been linked together could be separated by a chapter or verse.

The initial Greek was written in one continuous line. No chapters, verses or even punctuation at the end of sentences existed in the original Greek. All punctuation that appears in our modern translations was added, based on the interpretation of the translator.

Let's look at an example that shows potential misinterpretation due to the chapter/verse separators. When we read Matthew 10, Jesus is giving a long list of instructions to the disciples before He sends them out. He tells them to preach the Gospel, heal the sick, and cast out demons; He warns about false teachers, potential rewards and much more. After these instructions in chapter 10, the chapter break occurs and goes to Matthew 11:1. Following is the first verse of chapter 11.

> **Matthew 11:1** — Now it came to pass, when <u>Jesus finished commanding His twelve disciples</u>, that He departed from there to teach and to preach in their cities.

Do you see "Jesus finished commanding His twelve disciples" in 11:1? All of the commands referenced in 11:1 were given in Matthew 10. Matthew 11:1 can give the impression that Jesus' commands were a separate unknown event because of the separation in the chapters. You may be wondering why this is significant. Matthew 28 is why.

> **Matthew 28:19-20** — [19] <u>Go therefore and make disciples</u> of all the nations, baptizing them in the name of the Father and of the Son and of the Holy Spirit,[20] <u>teaching them to observe all things that I have commanded you</u>; and lo, I am with you always, *even* to the end of the age. Amen.

Those commands are important, because later in Matthew 28:19-20 Jesus instructed them to make disciples and teach His commands to those new disciples. This is followed by the new disciples making more disciples and again teaching them Jesus' commands. Repeat until the Gospel is preached to every creature! What commands are the new disciples supposed to be taught? All of Jesus' commands, including those in Matthew 10. This applies to us as Jesus' disciples today!

Punctuation is another feature that man added to the Bible, and it can cause misinterpretation, too. Let's look at a humorous example of how punctuation placement can alter meaning.

> Original words without punctuation:
> *Woman without her man is nothing.*
>
> How a man might punctuate the statement:
> *Woman, without her man, is nothing.*
>
> How a woman might punctuate the statement:
> *Woman: without her, man is nothing.*

A few commas can totally change the meaning, can't they? Punctuation can make a BIG difference in our interpretation. Now let's look at a biblical example. Luke 23:42-43 is part of the conversation between Jesus and the thief while they are being crucified.

Luke 23:42-43 — ⁴² Then he *(the thief)* said to Jesus, "Lord, remember me when You come into Your kingdom." ⁴³ And Jesus said to him, "<u>Assuredly, I say to you, today you will be with Me in Paradise.</u>"

Luke 23:43 has been a source of confusion for some because the Bible clearly states that Jesus died and was in the grave that day, not in paradise. Some say it was figurative, and some say that the paradise Jesus was referring to was some other heaven. The truth is that we should not draw conclusions where there is lack of information. The Greek uses no punctuation or verse separators, so in English, Jesus' statement could look like this:

Luke 23:43b — Assuredly I say to you today you will be with Me in Paradise

What would happen if the comma was placed *after* the word, *today?*

Luke 23:43b — Assuredly I say to you today, you will be with Me in Paradise

Do you see how the meaning changed? The second version implies that Jesus is saying that as of today, the thief can be assured that he will be with Jesus in paradise. Which meaning is correct? We don't actually know from this single verse. If we look up the Greek words and substitute their meanings, Jesus' statement *could* look like this (note that this is how it *may* have appeared in the Greek, not an authorized translation):

Luke 23:43b — Amen I am saying to you today with me you will be in the paradise

Unfortunately, substituting the Greek still does not make it clear in this case. At this point we look for other clues.

As we read through the Gospels, we look for patterns in how Jesus spoke. Just like you and me, Jesus had some favorite ways to structure His sentences when making a point. When Jesus wanted to emphasize a point, He often began His statements with, "*Assuredly* I say to you," or "*Verily, verily*, I say unto you." He uses this phrase numerous times in the Gospels.

We can then perform a *keyword search to locate all the times that Jesus began a statement with this phrase, and there were a lot! In nearly every case, there was a break in thought after the phrase, "Assuredly I say to you." This bit of detective work tells us that when we are studying a verse like Luke 23:43, we can use Jesus' usual pattern of speech to make a more educated deduction that the comma should be placed before the word *today* to bring across the correct meaning.

*Later in this book, we give detailed instructions for how to do a keyword search.

In the end, for verses like Luke 23:43, we look for the main thought and move on. Jesus told the thief that he would be in paradise. It would be wonderful to know exactly what went on behind the scenes after Jesus and the thief died, but we shouldn't make a doctrine out of this passage or any single passage of Scripture.

This is what we need to realize: the original Greek had no punctuation, and punctuation placement can alter our understanding of a Scripture. If a Scripture is unclear, study the passage without any punctuation or verse/chapter separations. Regardless, we shouldn't make a doctrine out of this passage or any single passage of Scripture.

Study Note: Here's an interesting exercise. If you are studying a short book like Colossians, copy and paste all the verses from an online Bible into a word processing program like *Microsoft Word*. Eliminate all the chapter and verse numbers, along with all separators like carriage returns and all punctuation like commas and periods. Read the chapters again. We aim to read with a fresh look at the Scripture like we have never seen it before! Optional: For a different point of view, additionally remove all capitalization from the text (this is easy to do in a word processing application like *Microsoft Word*), and then insert punctuation, like commas and periods, where you think they should go.

Chapter 6:
Power Tools for Bible Study

This is one of our favorite chapters in this book because we enjoy using technology while we study! These resources are not required but they help us to accomplish much more in a shorter time. If you're not tech savvy, do not let yourself become intimidated by the techniques in this chapter. Simply dive in and start swimming.

SOME FAVORITE BIBLE STUDY RESOURCES

We have already made the point that the main message of the Bible is simple. God wants everyone to be able to understand it. To know the basics, we need nothing more. Having said that, we will now discuss some of the power tools we like to use during Bible study. Why do we use them? Quite simply, they make Bible study more interesting and fun.

With these Bible study companions, you will be well armed for serious research! I have used these tools to answer some of the questions that pop into my head during study, and I have also used them to check the validity of teachings I have heard. Even better, many of these resources are FREE online! With today's technology, there are many great tools available that can make studying the Bible more fun and more effective.

In the following, we will reveal how you can integrate technology into your study time. There are Bible apps for smartphones and tablets as well as online search engines. I'll never forget my first time seeing verses come alive when I saw the treasure trove of online links and references to almost every notable biblical resource we know of. If you have primarily done Bible study using physical books, you will be amazed at what is available electronically. Whether you consider yourself tech savvy or not, there are easy-to-use sites that will make Bible study richer and more exciting.

The following resources are only a few of many available, but these are some of our current favorites. Under each tool, we have listed two of our favorite features or (in quotes) have listed the description assigned to the resource by the site. Please note that these resources have MANY valuable features that are not listed. There are those that even offer a mobile app version for a smartphone or tablet (some that we use to listen to the Bible via Bluetooth!). Some sites are simple to use and some require effort to learn but we encourage you to dive in and try them all. If you are completely new to Bible study, we have included some definitions and descriptions at the end of this chapter to aid in understanding. For even more definitions and examples (e.g., what is a lexicon?) use a search engine like Google.com.

FREE Resources
BibleGateway — www.biblegateway.com

- Easy-to-use online Bible. Many translations to choose from, including those in various languages.
- View side-by-side Bible translations. (up to 5!) Click on the **Add Parallel** button Try looking at a single verse or passage with these translations: NKJV, YLT, NASB, and AMP

Bible Study Tools.com — www.biblestudytools.com

- Links to Popular Resources (near the bottom), concordances, biblical dictionaries, Bible encyclopedias and historical documents to understand the meanings of words. It will even read the passage out loud to you.

- Handy reference shows the *Strong's Concordance* index number of any word that the mouse cursor hovers over. This makes it easy to see the original biblical root of any word in the KVJ.

Blue Letter Bible — www.blueletterbible.org

- Easy to use. Loads of information about a passage on a single web page. Enter a verse reference at the top, then click on the **Tools** button. The verse is then broken down into the original language word by word, along with a link to the *Strong's* entry and the root word along with a pronunciation.
- Quickly access *Vine's Expository Dictionary*, view all the ways the verse was translated in the KJV, Bible Usage outline, *Strong's Definitions*, *Thayer's Greek Lexicon*, and list of every verse that contains that Greek word.

Scripture 4 All — www.scripture4all.org

- Hebrew-English/Greek-English Interlinear pdf Bible
- Free Interlinear Scripture Analyzer download (link available from site above). This is a terrific tool to see not only the original root words but add parallel translations as well.

Study Bible — www.studybible.info

- Slightly more challenging to use but very powerful. Begin by entering a verse reference in the top search bar and select **Interlinear Greek** or **Hebrew**. This results in a breakdown of the verse with a wonderful assortment of cross references and parallel study options.
- From the verse view, click on a *Strong's* number to see the Greek lexicon (such as G1411: *dunamis*). The resulting page links to an amazing amount of information, too much to list here. This site has by far the most direct resource links we have seen on any site and it's all FREE!

Studylight — www.studylight.org

- "Original Language Tools" Archives on the Greek, Hebrew and Aramaic thought on words to understand the culture and usage of that word

- "Historical Writing" Before Jesus and after Jesus. Early Church Fathers and Denomination History

Treasury of Scripture Knowledge

thetreasuryofscriptureknowledge.com Also available as a hard cover book by R.A. Torrey

- Huge compilation of over 500,000 Scripture references and parallel passages
- "Reveals how Scripture interprets itself in every important verse, topic and word."

Webster's 1828 American Dictionary of the English Language
online edition — webstersdictionary1828.com

- At almost 200 years old, this dictionary helps us to understand the definitions of English words used by the translators of the King James version (KJV) of the Bible.
- This resource can be freely downloaded to your cell phone, also available in hard copy book.

Recommended Resources for Purchase

Dake's Annotated Reference Bible (KJV) by Finis Jennings Dake

- More challenging to use, but worth the effort. Systematic and logical, comprehensive layout that took the author over 100,000 hours to compile. Note that the print is very small in the standard edition. Consider getting the large print.
- "The purpose of this work is to give in ONE volume the helps a student of the Bible needs from many books — Bible Commentaries, Atlas, Dictionary, complete Concordance, Dispensational Truth, Topical Text Book, Bible Syntheses, Doctrines, Prophetic Studies, and others."

God's Plan for Man by Finis Jennings Dake

- Written as an intensive 1 year, 52-week Bible school course, but excellent as a topical reference guide.
- "A library of Bible knowledge in compact form, it contains more than 10,000 subjects, sermon outlines, and questions fully

answered — all supported and proved by more than 33,000 references to Scripture passages. Nothing is left to human reasoning alone, or proved by human authority. The Bible is recognized as its own interpreter, and there is a continual emphasis on 'rightly dividing the word of truth.'"

The Life of Christ in Stereo: The Four Gospels Speak in Harmony by Johnston M. Cheney

- All four gospels combined in historical sequence makes it easy to see the parallel stories of Jesus.

- "The Purpose of This Harmony — THE LIFE OF CHRIST IN STEREO is a meticulous combination of the four Gospels which seeks to bring into stereo-scopic relief the four dimensional portrayal of Christ and His ministry. It presents a composite portrait of the One Who is the Central Personality of history, tracing the events of His ministry in chronological order, without omission of the smallest detail."

The New Testament: An Expanded Translation
by Kenneth Wuest

- One of our favorite ways to quickly get an understanding of the New Testament Greek. No Greek knowledge or computer skills required!

- This Bible was written as a meaning-for-meaning interpretation instead of translating words and phrases. The result is a Bible which uses as many words as necessary to convey each thought from the Greek into English. In other words, it is written how Wuest determined that a Greek person reading the New Testament in the Greek language at the time of Jesus would understand it as written in English in the 1950s and 60s. An interesting feature is that the usual verse separations are converted into verse ranges, and chapter numbers are given as Roman numerals.

THE MIGHTY KEY WORD SEARCH

Key word searches are a quick way to learn about a biblical topic. We use this method A LOT. *BibleGateway* and other online tools make searching the Bible for keywords very easy. Start with a good translation before beginning the search. Many online study tools default to NIV, so make sure to change the selection to one of the recommended translations.

A key word search involves typing a word into a search box. An application then searches for every instance of that word throughout the specified area of the Bible and returns a list of all the matching verses. Typing in a search word is very simple, and it is remarkably effective in helping to get wonderful revelation from God's Word. Fifty years ago, study would have required a *Strong's Concordance* to find the verse references, followed by looking up the verses by hand. Now, with online search utilities, this is much easier and faster. We can find hundreds of verses in seconds and quickly copy them all into a file to begin sorting them.

Example

Let's suppose that we want to study what the Bible says about *grace* and *works*.

We have two key words in this case: *grace* and *works*. In this example, we demonstrate how to perform a key word search for verses about *works* because this search will allow us to show you a few more tricks. We will limit the search to New Testament only.

1. Select one of the recommended translations.

2. Using *BibleGateway* (or another search utility), locate the **Search** box.

3. In the **Search** box, enter a shortened version of the word, in this case: *work*. Note that if we enter *work* we get 720 verses, but *works* only appears in 238 verses. The search for *work* will return verses that include variations such as *worked, working, works, handiwork*, and so on. We know that only some of the verses that contain the word *work* are what we are looking for, but we want our search results to include variations of the word so that we don't miss what we are looking for.

4. Brainstorm a list of additional words to search. More words may come to mind after reading some of the verses from the initial search results of *work*.

   a. Words related to the concept of *works* such as *do, doing, fruit,* etc.

   b. Synonyms of *work* (mean the same) such as *labor* (or *labour*), *deeds*, *toil* and *persevere*

   c. Antonyms of *work* (opposite of) such as *idle, lazy*.

5. Assess which verses seem applicable, then copy and paste them into a word processing document or spreadsheet (such as *Microsoft Word* or *Excel*).

6. In your new document, sort the verses into categories. Determine how you will categorize the verses according to what seems logical to you. Here are some ideas:

   a. Group by headings such as *Dead works*, *Works of Obedience*, *Rewards*, *Spiritual Fruit*, and *Miscellaneous*.

   b. (Optional) If the verse supports your current belief, make it blue. If the verse goes against your current belief, make it red

Here's another example from our past that incorporates a key word search with a twist. At one point, we were doing some research and I recalled the word *infirmity* appeared in a verse, but we couldn't remember where (it was in Romans 6:19). Using *BibleGateway*, we performed a keyword search for the word *infirmity* in the NASB but the search results did not display Romans 6:19! Here's why.

Romans 6:19a (KJV) I speak after the manner of men because of the <u>infirmity</u> of your flesh:

Romans 6:19a (NASB) I am speaking in human terms because of the <u>weakness</u> of your flesh.

Notice that the King James Version (KJV) above uses the word *infirmity*, and the New American Standard (NASB) uses the term *weakness* instead. To locate this passage using the keyword, *infirmity*, we would have to search in the correct Bible <u>translation</u>. The problem is that most of the time I don't know what version to search because I have learned verses from various translations throughout my life.

Here is what we did. The trick is to use a search engine that doesn't rely on the translation. I used an internet search engine like *Google.com* to look for Bible verses that contained the word *infirmity*. *Google* will return many unrelated websites, but it will also search many Bible translations at the same time, which is what we wanted. *BibleGateway* and other online Bible websites have powerful features for performing these kinds of advanced searches, but a site like *Google* is usually the fastest and easiest. Once *Google* returns the Scripture reference we are looking for, we can locate it in our Bible in the correct translation to read it in context and do more detailed study.

> [Kevin] Sometimes the verse that I'm looking for doesn't even exist! One time I was doing a study on why God made mankind. I tried doing a keyword search to find the verse that says mankind was *made to worship*. I assumed because I had heard that phrase for years — even in Christian songs — that it was in the Bible. It's not! I highly recommend doing a study to see why we were created. I was really surprised at what I found.

Word Definitions Matter

Language is a complex thing. The same word could mean something different to you and me, and that word could also mean something different to a person living in the 1600's versus someone living today. The same English word may have a different understood meaning across cultures such as the United States, Great Britain, Kenya and many English-speakers around the world.

The understood meaning of words can affect how we interpret what the Bible means. For example, the original King James version of the Bible was written in the early 1600's. However, the King James we read today is not the 1611 version. That version of the Bible was last revised in 1769. The understood meaning of some words has changed over the course of 400 years.

Word definitions are very important! Sometimes people have interpreted a particular word in Scripture differently than the original intent, then went on to build an entire belief system on it. It's easy to assume that we know what a word means. Sometimes we don't even realize that the definition in our minds is not the same as the meaning of the original word. For example, the word, *flesh* in Scripture sometimes means skin, but it can also mean a worldly or sinful nature.

The first step is just realizing that we should verify definitions, especially in verses that seem to go against the natural flow of other passages we have read. In other words, if a verse does not seem to agree with other verses you have read, then simply look up the meanings of the key words in a reputable, (preferably older) dictionary. When several of the older translations (e.g., KJV) were created, the translators used terminology that was relevant at that time.

Webster's 1828 American Dictionary* of the English Language is a great resource for those reading the King James version (KJV) of the Bible. This dictionary was not written precisely when the KJV was published, but it gets us much closer than a modern dictionary and our contemporary use of words. For our example we will continue with Romans 6:19.

Romans 6:19 (KJV) — I speak after the manner of men because of the <u>infirmity</u> of your flesh: for as ye have yielded your members servants to uncleanness and to iniquity unto iniquity; even so now yield your members servants to righteousness unto holiness.

In Romans 6:19 we see the word *infirmity* in the phrase *infirmity of your flesh*. When I read the word *infirmity* I would think that it means sickness. I would then understand this verse to be discussing sickness in the body as a result of sin. However, when I looked up the word *infirmity* in the dictionary, the definition isn't quite what I thought.

Common Usage of Word *Infirmity*: Sickness or Disease

Definition of *Infirmity* as given in the *Webster's 1828 Dictionary* (According to entry in webstersdictionary1828.com)

- Unsound or unhealthy state of the body; weakness; feebleness. Old age is subject to infirmities.
- Weakness of mind; failing; fault; foible. A friend should bear a friend's infirmities.
- Weakness of resolution
- Any particular disease; malady; applied rather to chronic, than to violent diseases
- Defect; imperfection; weakness; as in the infirmities of a constitution of government.

From this definition, we find that *infirmity* can mean *sickness*, but it also means *weakness*. Please note that even though the dictionary may show five different meanings for *infirmity*, not all of those definitions apply to how the word is being used in a passage.

Let's look at the New American Standard version (NASB) of Romans 6:19.

> **Romans 6:19 (NASB)** — I am speaking in human terms because of the <u>weakness</u> of your flesh. For just as you presented your members as slaves to impurity and to lawlessness, resulting in further lawlessness, so now present your members as slaves to righteousness, resulting in sanctification.

Note that the NASB uses the term *weakness* instead of *infirmity*. This word changes the verse's meaning significantly! *Weakness of your flesh* refers to the tendency of people to succumb to their earthly/worldly desires. In this passage the writer is encouraging people to be just as dedicated to righteousness as they used to be slaves to unrighteousness.

How do we know if the word *infirmity* in Romans 6:19 (KJV) refers to *sickness* or *weakness*? It helps to look at definitions from reputable dictionaries published close to the same time period. Another good practice is to read the passage in several recommended translations of the Bible as we did above. This is easy to do using the parallel translation feature on *BibleGateway* and other online Bible sites. In *BibleGateway*, we can read up to five selected translations side by side.

Here's another interesting example. The 1599 Geneva Bible (GNV) published in 1560 was one of the most significant and respected English translations of its time. In fact, it was one of the versions the Pilgrims took to America on the Mayflower and was consider the first English study Bible ever written.

The King James version (KJV) followed about 51 years later in 1611, although the King James we read today is from the 1769 revision. I encourage you to look at the 1611 version of the King James online (available on *BibleGateway*). It's very interesting! The New King James (NKJV) was commissioned in 1975 as a contemporary version of the King James which modified the wording to more closely align with modern language conventions. The New American Standard Bible (NASB) was the most current of our selection, published in 1995.

In Genesis 3:7 below, the versions are listed with the oldest translation first. Notice how the underlined word changes to reflect the time in which it was written. This progression illustrates how the word has been translated from the same Hebrew word (*chagor*), but the translation was changed to better align with the current understanding and usage of the word.

1599 Geneva Bible (GNV)

Then the eyes of them both were opened, and they knew that they were naked, and they sewed fig tree leaves together, and made themselves <u>breeches</u>.

King James Version (KJV)

And the eyes of them both were opened, and they knew that they were naked; and they sewed fig leaves together, and made themselves <u>aprons</u>.

New King James Version (NKJV)
Then the eyes of both of them were opened, and they knew that they were naked; and they sewed fig leaves together and made themselves <u>coverings</u>.

New American Standard (NASB)
Then the eyes of both of them were opened, and they knew that they were naked; and they sewed fig leaves together and made themselves <u>loin coverings</u>.

<u>IMPORTANT NOTE</u>: In reputable translations, the Bible is very clear in its main doctrinal points. From Jesus coming to earth, dying for our sins and being raised from the dead, Jesus' commands, the gospel and the great commission are clear. Looking up the definitions of words is unlikely to change how we understand main points of Scripture, but it can help us to clarify and solidify our comprehension in areas we are making assumptions.

A Remarkably Easy Way to Study Using Biblical Greek and Hebrew

Listening to teaching, I was always in awe when I heard a minister talk about the meaning of an original Greek or Hebrew word in the Bible. I was convinced that they must have spent hundreds of hours studying the language in seminary. While that may be true for some, technology has made it very simple to study the Bible in the original languages. Today, there are definite advantages to having formal training, but it is amazing how much depth God can show people like you and me with only the internet and a little practice. YOU CAN DO IT!

It is well worth the effort of learning how to study the Bible in its original language. Early Old Testament manuscripts were initially written in Hebrew and Chaldean, and the New Testament was initially written in biblical Greek. When the New Testament was translated from biblical Greek into our native language, there was not always a perfect fit in meaning from one language to the other in a word-for-word translation.

Some Greek and Hebrew words simply do not translate precisely into English, so the translators had to choose the words they felt expressed the closest meaning. This gave room for mistakes. The person translating the Scripture may have been taught to believe a certain way about a biblical topic. As a result, the translation may show this bias. This does NOT mean that the Bible in the original language is wrong; it just means that a mistake was made in translating. Looking at the Hebrew and Greek helps to bypass this discrepancy and allows us to understand the original intent more clearly.

Here is a basic rule of thumb. If a verse does not make sense or seems to disagree with other Scripture, reading it in context will almost always make it clear. If it is still unclear, then looking at the original Greek or Hebrew word and its definition should provide clarification. In fact, I often look at the Greek or Hebrew out of curiosity. I think you will find it interesting and easy, too. Follow along as we go through an example.

Let's suppose that we are studying God's *power* and how it works in and through us. We come across the verse Luke 10:19.

Luke 10:19 (KJV) — Behold, I give unto you **power** to tread on serpents and scorpions, and over all the **power** of the enemy: and nothing shall by any means hurt you.

The word *power* in this passage is used twice: both the power Jesus has given us and the power of the enemy. Jesus says that we have power over the enemy's power. How does that work? We will use Luke 10:19, the King James version, because this is the very study that we were doing when we first learned how to look at the original Greek.

To bring a better understanding to this verse, use the following steps to look up both instances of the word, *power* in the Greek.

1. Go to *www.blueletterbible.org*.

2. Enter **Luke 10:19** in the search box and specify **King James Version (KJV)**.

3. Click the magnifying glass to execute the search.

4. The entire chapter of Luke 10 appears. Select **Luke 10:19** by clicking on the reference.

5. A window appears with a tab for each type of reference material. Ensure that **Interlinear** is selected. Locate the first occurrence of the word *power*. Click on the *Strong's* **G1849** link next to it.

6. The lexicon opens to show that in this instance, *power* was translated from the Greek word *exousia*. Under **Outline of Biblical Usage**, read the entries for this word.

7. In your journal, take note of what *exousia* means, with an emphasis on *authority*.

8. Scroll down further on the page to see the **Concordance Results Using KJV**. Look through this section to see how the same original word, *exousia* was translated in other passages.

9. In your browser, click the **Back** button to return to the verse (save time by opening the link in a new tab)

10. Locate the second occurrence of the word *power*. Notice that *power* in this case was translated from an entirely different Greek word. We know this because it has a different *Strong's* number. Click on the *Strong's* **G1411** link next to the word.

11. The lexicon opens to show that in this instance, *power* was translated from the Greek word *dunamis*. Under **Outline of Biblical Usage**, read the meaning of this word. In your journal, take note of what *power* means, with an emphasis on *ability*.

12. Return to the original Scripture. Read the passage aloud, substituting the definition of the Greek words for each instance of *power*.

    For example, we can say, "Behold, I give unto you ***authority*** to tread on serpents and scorpions, and over all the ***ability*** of the enemy: and nothing shall by any means hurt you."

13. Scroll down further on the page to see the **Concordance Results Using KJV**. Look through this section to see how the term is used in other passages.

What we have now seen is that in the KJV, two different Greek words were both translated into the same word: *power*. Jesus gave believers *authority* over all of the enemy's *ability*. Just as a policeman has authority that overrides a criminal's ability, the authority Jesus has given us overrides the ability of the enemy. From Acts 1:8 we know that we also have power (*dunamis*) from the Holy Spirit. This means that we have authority (*exousia*) and power (*dunamis*) through God. The enemy has some ability, but we have been given authority and power over it.

> **Acts 1:8** — But you shall receive power when the Holy Spirit has come upon you; and you shall be witnesses to Me in Jerusalem, and in all Judea and Samaria, and to the end of the earth.

After performing an extensive study on a passage using some of the techniques we have discussed so far, it is a very meaningful exercise to write the verse in your own words. Take key definitions and original Greek or Hebrew word meanings and write an expanded version of the passage, substituting some of the words with their meanings. Performing this exercise allows us to get a clearer picture of what the verse is saying and can bring our revelation of it to an entirely different level.

In our example we looked up definitions for the original Greek words. This is an easy and powerful method to dig deeper in Bible study, but it doesn't stop there. Some scholars and theologians also analyze the grammar of the Greek to get an even better understanding. Looking up the definitions is great, but knowing the grammar is even better. Understanding the grammar can take a lot of study and education, but many who have put in the time and effort have been well-rewarded.

WHAT IS A LEXICON? AND OTHER RESOURCE DEFINITIONS

Concordance: Alphabetized list of all the words in the Bible and the references (book/chapter/verse) to locate them. One of the most widely used in the United States is the *Strong's Exhaustive Concordance of the Bible*.

Context: The setting and situation surrounding an event which helps the reader to more fully understand what they are reading.

Cross-reference: In literature, a reference to another part of text (or resource) on the same topic

Hermaneutics: A comprehensive study of Biblical interpretation

Interlinear Bible: A Bible that shows the English translation along with the corresponding Hebrew or Greek word(s). Many online Bible resources include an Interlinear Greek New Testament and an Interlinear Hebrew Old Testament.

Lexicon: A dictionary; a resource to determine the meaning of words such as a Hebrew lexicon or a Greek lexicon. Some of the most notable online are *Thayer's Greek Lexicon of the New Testament* (referenced in some resources as *Thayer's*) and *Liddell and Scott Greek-English Lexicon (LSJ Gloss)*.

Strong's Concordance of the Bible: *Strong's Concordance* is an index of every word appearing in the Bible. Each original language word was assigned a number (known as the "Strong's Number"). This Strong's number makes it easy to link to the original Hebrew or Greek word for further study. We usually see a letter prefix before the number – either *H* or *G*. This indicating that the particular word originated in either Hebrew or Greek, Old or New Testament.

Chapter 7: Putting It All Together

It is one thing to read about Bible study methods and techniques and quite another to utilize them during your time in God's Word. Remember that they may not seem natural at first, but with a little practice you will develop your own system of study that works well for you.

You may have never read the Bible without a devotional aid by your side, but there is nothing like studying the Bible with no one to interject except the Holy Spirit. You may have never read the Bible without a devotional aid by your side, but there is nothing like studying the Bible with no one to interject except the Holy Spirit. Even when we use online tools, we are not interested in another person's opinion about how a passage should be interpreted. We seek to know what God Himself is telling us through His Word.

In this chapter, we share how other people study the Bible in the way that works best for them. Some of these people are pastors and teachers, but not all. We put these personal examples in here to inspire you to try some new techniques and to show you that you don't need to go to seminary to be able to get amazing revelation from God and disciple others to do the same.

SUMMARY OF TIPS TO UNDERSTAND A SCRIPTURE

When I read books with a lot of techniques I appreciate a summary page that puts everything together. It is easier to remember one page than 100. For that reason, here is a summary for you.

1. Pray before and after Bible study. Ask for understanding and thank God for the revelation He has given.
2. Seek truth and be open to finding out you have had wrong beliefs.
    a. Do not piece Scripture together to fit your belief system.
    b. Decide to follow the evidence and truth
3. Read aloud, slowly
    a. Make certain to clearly say each word
    b. Read the verse emphasizing the first word, then repeat, emphasizing the subsequent word each time until all words have been emphasized.
4. Using a dictionary, look up the definitions of key words in a passage.
    a. We sometimes have a preconceived idea about a word that makes a big difference in the verse's meaning (such as *infirmity*).
    b. Understand the terminology used at the time the translation was written may not have the same meaning today.
5. Focus on understanding the verse as part of the entire passage, chapter and book. Read at least three verses before and three verses after to capture the context.
6. Ask questions and write down the answers for the Scripture you are studying (*Who*, *What*, *When*, *Where*, *Why*, and *How*).
7. Look up the passage using an Interlinear Greek New Testament or Hebrew Old Testament. Most online resources have clickable links for each word for deeper study.
8. From the Interlinear, click on key words (usually through the *Strong's* lexicon number such as *G3588* or *H2290*) to see the definitions of the original words.
9. Find other verses that have that same Greek or Hebrew word in them. Investigate how the word is used in other passages.
10. Rewrite the verse, substituting the definitions for the key words.

The techniques in this list are not the end, they are only the beginning. You will develop your own style of study that works best for you, combining methods we have discussed in this book and adding some of your own.

In the following sections, we share some personal styles of Bible study that integrate the techniques in this book in various ways. By sharing these processes, our goal is to inspire ideas about what methods will work best for you.

CAROL TRAVIS — PREPARING TO PREACH

(C. Travis, personal communication April 11, 2017)

I am a mother, a grandmother, and a pastor. Every week I study God's Word to put together a teaching for my congregation. This is how I do it:

1. IMPORTANT — I talk to Holy Spirit. He is the Teacher. If there is something that interests me, I ask Him to help me search it out. (If I am excited about a subject, it is easy to pass on my enthusiasm.)

2. I start with the concordance in the back of my Bible. If I can find a word related to the subject, I look up the Scripture and check for any cross-references in the margin. I follow the "thread" to all the verses that I find.

3. I use an online concordance and search for the topic, usually using two or three different translations. Sometimes I look up key words in an online Bible dictionary.

4. At this point, Holy Spirit puts together an outline and all the verses just seem to fit together effortlessly. Now we can "dig in" to the wonderful banquet Holy Spirit has prepared!

5. <u>Application is key</u> — How do these scriptures apply to my life? This is where Holy Spirit reveals personal application which may be different for each person involved.

Filling our mind with Bible facts is one thing; receiving nuggets of gold from Holy Spirit is another. Bible study without Holy Spirit and without application is just an exercise of the brain. Bible study with Holy Spirit and application is a life changing experience — that lasts a lifetime!

KATHY'S FAVORITE — SHORT AND SWEET

When I sit down to spend time with God, I usually begin with a deep breath, clear away the multitude of daily "to-do's" on my mind, and focus on God. Sometimes I'll start by asking God what He wants to tell me through His Word and telling Him how much I love Him. I'm reverent but informal, as though I'm having a conversation with someone I admire and respect deeply. If there are still pressing issues on my mind I pray about them, giving them to Him. I'm so glad He told us to cast our cares on Him because He cares for us! I rely on Him for encouragement, motivation and inspiration.

For me, Bible *study* is a different activity than simply *reading* the Bible. When I read the Bible, I usually select a book, start at the beginning and continue for a few chapters. However, when I study, I'm looking for answers to questions I have about a particular topic. I begin by doing a keyword search using an online Bible site like *BibleGateway*. I am a researcher at heart, so oftentimes I sift through the results and pick only two or three passages that seem to lead in the right direction and begin to study them in depth.

Most of the time, I study only one verse in detail. I expand my reading area to get the context of the verse, and then try to summarize the thoughts the writer was trying to convey. I look up all the cross references from my chosen passage and look at any parallel passages (if it is one of the Gospel accounts). Reading through slowly, I try to notice all the explicit and implied absolutes in the verse and if it is a promise from God, I determine what that promise is. If it is a command, am I following it? How does this passage relate to me in my life?

If this promise from God is something that I want to really impress in my mind, I read it out loud, emphasizing a different word every time. I have found this works well to help me *own* the promise God has made with the added benefit of helping me to memorize Scripture. Another great way to memorize Scripture is to go over memory verses with family members in the car. While I am driving I can't look at the verse, so I *have* to memorize it!

Because I enjoy using Bible **power tools**, I then look up the passage I'm studying using the Interlinear Greek or Hebrew text online using a site like *studybible.info*. From there, I click on key words in the passage and look at the definitions of those words. It's interesting to me to see how the same Greek or Hebrew word was translated in other passages as well. This feature often gives me additional cross references that I hadn't found before. I substitute the key words in the verse with the appropriate definitions and read it again.

If I want to go even further, I look up the passage in the *Wuest Bible* (for New Testament) or the *Dake Annotated Reference Bible*. These resources can introduce some additional human bias, so I try to look at these books only after I have allotted time for God to talk to me directly about them. In my journal, I like to write down the verse, the promise, any interesting cross references, and what the Holy Spirit showed me through my study time.

I also write down any questions that I still want answers to. I'm not shy about asking questions; I have lists of them written in my journal. Lots of times when the answers come I don't have my journal, but I have found that entering them in my phone helps me recall them later.

Lately, I have been trying to meditate on the things God has shown me and find ways to share them with others, whether it is in person at a sporting event or on social media. Not only does this solidify the principles in my own mind, but I know that if God took the time to show me, I can glorify and honor Him by sharing to help encourage someone else.

LISA SCHERBENSKE — STUDYING BOOK BY BOOK

(L. Scherbenske, personal communication April 14, 2017)

I tend to study the Bible one book at a time. Because I had never actually finished the entire Old Testament until recently, I found it easier to read it book by book, because that is how I had studied the New Testament. I was struggling through some of the chapters in the Old Testament, so I purchased a set of CDs and also listened on my electronic device as I read along with it in my Bible. Listening to the Bible also helped with words that were difficult to pronounce.

For me, the most important key to studying The Word is going slowly and repeating each verse several times while asking God for wisdom as He reveals Himself through the words. Knowing this is not a foot race or a checklist for my day, but a relationship, gave me permission to be more intentional, involved and tuned into what God had to say to me personally. I don't know how many times I'd be asking God a question and then I'd open my Bible and right there in front of me was the answer!

I still study the Bible going through one book at a time, but probably my favorite way to read it is just sitting quietly in worship, prayer and conversing, asking questions and listening to Him answer. In those moments, He often points out a scripture, I look it up and take notes, and sometimes I have even more questions!

Hunger for His Word started to grow in me as I began to actually believe and act upon what was written and how He spoke to me. When He revealed to me the words, "by His stripes we are healed" in Isaiah 53, it meant He paid for our healing and much more at the cross. This totally changed how I viewed the nature of God and the depth of His love for me.

When I understood what He meant when He said; "Most assuredly, I say to you, he who believes in Me, the works that I do he will do also; and greater works than these he will do, because I go to My Father" in John 14:12, I started to see who I was in Him and He began speaking to me about my identity in Christ Jesus, who I was and what I had because of His life, death and resurrection. I found myself becoming much bolder in my daily walk. But it was the power of the Holy Spirit that was the key ingredient behind my actions and the words that I spoke.

The next thing I knew I was experiencing His healing touch and many miracles began to follow. I began looking at the scriptures with new eyes, His love was almost overwhelming and His truths began to leap off the pages and manifest in my daily life. This is where I believe we move from studying the Bible or gathering information/knowledge to really living it! The Word gets cemented into our hearts and is so full that it feels like it just must naturally leak out of us!

In closing, my hope is that you will discover the deep, deep love that Jesus has for you, through His Word and through the power of the Holy Spirit. As we renew our minds with The Word our thoughts about who God is and who we are will change. We will be able to see ourselves more clearly how God sees us and we will discover the true nature and character of a God who had us in mind when He sent His only Son into the world to save us and to give us abundant life.

TODD MCNICHOLAS — DISCIPLE SOMEONE IN HOW TO STUDY THE BIBLE

(T. McNicholas, personal communication December 19, 2016)

3 Important Items

In real estate, there is a saying that there are 3 important items that everyone needs to know, "Location, Location, and Location." When it comes to reading and studying the Bible there are 3 important items that everyone needs to know, "Context, Context, and Context." This is particularly true when reading one of the letters such as Galatians, Ephesians, Philippians and Colossians.

Bible Study Guidelines

The following guidelines can help you and someone you are discipling to successfully read and study the Bible.

1. Read the teachings, account, prophecy, or letter all the way through. This is one way to help you obtain a general idea of what is being said and the issues being addressed.

2. Underline term(s) that reoccur throughout the book. Colored pencils or pens with multiple ink colors are great tools to use for this. For instance, you might use red to underline terms or themes that speak of the blood of Jesus and the remission of sins.

3. As you read, pay attention to the following items:

    a. Who is the audience? Who asked the question? Who is the letter written to? etc.

    b. What is being addressed?

    c. When did it occur? Immediately following a feast? Immediately following a miracle? etc.

    d. Why was this written? Why did Jesus say what He said? Why was this prophecy spoken? etc.

    e. How does the text apply to me?

Discipling Someone in How to Study the Bible

When discipling people it could be good to start them in one of the short letters in the New Testament.

I recommend Paul's letter to the Colossians. Why?

- It is only four chapters long.
- Paul wrote to people who had committed their lives to Jesus, but whom he had not met. So we can say that Paul wanted to be sure that the Colossians would be getting what they needed to know to live victorious Christian lives.
- The letter speaks of the supremacy of Christ, His involvement in creation, our deliverance from the power of darkness, our death to the old life and our new life in Jesus, and more.

Chapter 7: Putting It All Together

Kevin's Favorite — New Testament Review

This method is not difficult. In fact, it is very easy, but it does take a significant amount of time. It is a slow and methodical process that I use to complete study on a topic.

To do this you will need an audio version of the Bible, a notebook, pen, a word processing software like Microsoft Word and internet access. If you do not have an audio version of the Bible, you can certainly read it instead.

Start with a purpose — a subject or question. With a notebook and pen, listen to the entire New Testament starting at Matthew 1:1 and go through Revelation 22:21. This takes approximately 18 hours, so depending on my schedule I may have 15 minutes or 2 hours to listen at a sitting. I listen for <u>anything</u> that talks about that subject that I am studying and record it in my notebook. Any verse I hear that <u>supports</u> or <u>goes against</u> my current belief or understanding is written down.

My goal is to try to put aside all preconceptions, everything I have believed before and start with a clean slate, taking God's Word at face value. I need to be interested in what the Bible says more than what I currently believe. I need to seek Him and not worry about being wrong. In fact, I have NEVER done this on any topic and had my beliefs and understanding on that topic remain the same.

When you hear a Scripture that contains information on your subject, write down the verse references' chapter and a few key words. Sometimes I write a plus (+) or minus (—) in front of the verse, to designate that the verse supports or goes against my current belief. Always look for EVERYTHING that supports or goes against what you believe. You must do this process with an open mind if you want to find the truth.

Next, make an outline in Microsoft Word with headings and subheadings pertaining to your topic. Copy and paste the verses from *BibleGateway* under the headings and subheadings. Color-code the verses that support your current understanding in blue and the verses that seem to oppose your current understanding in red.

What I usually find is that nearly every verse agrees with the other verses on a topic. If a verse stands out and does not seem to agree, then make sure to read it in context. By reading in context, it is recommended to read at least three verses before and after the verse. Sometimes, the verse that I thought was talking about a specific subject was actually addressing something completely different, so I delete that verse from the outline.

> [Kevin] Not long ago I was preparing to talk to people and the *perfect* verse to support my point came to mind. To prepare, I was presenting what I found to my son, so I showed him how to read the verse in context. To my surprise, I found out the verse I wanted to use was not even talking about what I thought it did! My son not only learned how to read a verse in context but also realized that no matter how long someone has studied the Bible, they can make mistakes. We should always check and never assume that a teaching is biblically accurate.

After reading a verse in context, if you still feel that it disagrees with the other verses, select key words in the passage and look up their meanings in the original language. As you look up the meanings of the words, write out the verse, substituting the keywords with the meanings from the original language. The next step I take is to perform keyword searches to find additional information on the topic and add them into the outline. When searching, remember to enter a shortened version of the word (e.g., look up *work*, not *works* or *worked*). Repeat the search for similar words (such as *deeds*) and opposite words (such as *idle* or *rest*).

When I am really going after truth on a subject, I carry around a pen and small pocket sized notebook with me everywhere I go. It's almost comical because Kathy finds them stashed in vehicles, tucked under my computer monitor and other places. Any time the Holy Spirit shows me or tells me something I want to be able to write it down immediately! He uses so many ways! It seems like verses on that topic, past conversations, songs, things people say, things said on the radio or in sermons will somehow refer to the topic I am pursuing. These notes have been treasures to me. The book you are reading right now came in part from things I scribbled into those little notebooks. Just remember to copy them all into a big notebook or word processing document so you do not lose them.

Sometimes I want to go to the next level with a topic. With my mind focused on that topic, I select a colored pen or Bible highlighter and read through the entire New Testament, searching for answers on that topic. After searching in the New Testament, certain topics can really benefit from digging into the Old Testament. I can say with confidence that you will realize verses and truth on that topic that you had never seen before. The amount of highlighting is wild.

I realize that this process seems long, but it has really benefitted my growth. I like to follow a process and once you find a process that works well for you, keep it up!

Here's a key: if we are not truly open to finding out we are wrong, then we are NOT interested in what the truth really is. If we aren't open to being wrong, we are only pursuing information to prove that we are right so that we do not have to change or admit that we were wrong. If there is one thing that I have learned in the last 10 years is that my beliefs were wrong at times. God worked on me and I chose to be open to His truth. I decided to believe it and do what it says; it was at that point when biblical truth really opened up for me. I understood the Bible better and now I take pleasure in listening to the Bible, reading it and most importantly, discovering and applying the truths I find in my life.

BOB SPURLOCK — UNDERSTAND THE OLD TESTAMENT

(R. Spurlock, personal communication December 30, 2016)

<u>How I Study the Bible</u> by Bob Spurlock of Wings of Calvary Ministries

The Bible is the Word of God. What we know as the Old Testament, and specifically what we know as the Torah, is the foundation for all other revelation. Without it the very sacrifice of Christ would have no context, no meaning. This is why Jesus said that not even one "jot" (the smallest Hebrew letter) nor one "tittle" (the traditional and formal flourish on top of Hebrew letters used in writing Scripture) would pass away until all was fulfilled. Even our dearest Christian doctrines, for the diligent student, are fully laid out in the Old Testament.

How can I say that? I didn't say it. The apostle Paul said it in 2 Timothy 3:14-17. Speaking to his spiritual son Timothy, he said this: "all Scripture is useful, and able to thoroughly equip the man of God for every good work." The Scripture Paul had then and what he was referring to were those same scriptures Jesus used: the Torah, the Prophets and the Writings (Tanach in Hebrew).

Today we call these books the Old Testament, but it was actually the 2nd century heretic Marcion who coined that term for the collection of 37 books we know as: Genesis to Malachi. Paul's statement to Timothy establishes that the importance of this foundational part of God's Word contains instruction in how to fulfill every command or desire Jesus passed on to His disciples: "Go to all the World; make disciples; heal the sick, raise the dead, cast out demons."

With that established, I believe the Scriptures in their original language and writing to be a perfectly accurate recounting of God's heart for us and for the whole world. There are no perfect translations, and even our oldest existing "original language" manuscripts contain a few inconsistencies. But, in spite of all that, the Scriptures we have are still able, as Paul said, to "make you wise unto salvation." For that reason alone, they are worthy of study. They are revelations of Christ, who "has the words of Life."

A few rules:

1. The Bible is first meant to be taken literally and I try to do that wherever possible by always comparing Scripture with itself.
2. I study from its literary historical context — what did the original author intend for his original audience to understand?
3. Use a concordance for understanding the meaning and nuances of original words. It doesn't take a Bible language scholar to use these simple tools.
4. Study inductively (avoid commentaries). Let the Word reveal and interpret itself.
5. Make it a daily habit and see it as an adventure with God — ask His help.
6. Write down what you learn.

Suggestions for studying the Torah:

- Start in Genesis and read the story. Don't get bogged down in the details. Just read the stories.
- When reading Psalms, understand that they are songs. Understand that you are singing real emotions expressed in the context of true worship.
- Re-write the Psalms with definitions from the Hebrew Bible dictionary.
- Know that the Torah is the foundation upon which the rest of Biblical revelation rests. It will help you to place in context the things that happen in the Gospels.
- The Bible is logical. Line upon line and precept upon precept.

Chapter 8: Next Steps

Jesus' plan for teaching His disciples involved a strategy to reach the entire world. He told them to teach others what He had taught them. It's easy for us to think it is someone else's job to spread the Gospel, but Jesus told us to do it. We are to be His ambassadors, His word, His hands and feet. We are to take what we have been given and be Jesus in this world.

Making Disciples

Sharing God's Word with other people is exciting, but it can be difficult to know where to start. I was amazed at how much I learned myself when I began to share with others! With just a little bit of studying you will have A LOT to share with others.

> [Kathy] Before I share some of the revelation God has shown me with other people, the enemy often tries to place thoughts of doubt in my mind such as, "Why would anyone want to listen to what I have to share?" or "What if they disagree with me or prove me wrong?"
>
> God has called us to be obedient. Jesus also stated the Golden Rule in Matthew 7:12, that whatever we would want others to do for us is what we should do for them. When I think back to where I was only a few years ago, I would have been so grateful for someone to share with me what I know now. Discipling another person isn't just a command, it's a form of worship and sacrifice to our God. Have courage, step out and grow.

The following are some ideas to help prepare for sharing the Bible with another person. The topic can be *anything* God has been showing you through the Bible. Here's a tip: choose a topic that is positive and exciting for you. If you're passionate about something, it's a lot easier and more fun to talk about. If it is positive, we share with joy, not criticism or complaining. Enthusiasm and optimism are contagious, and there are a lot of God's promises to be glad about!

1. To prepare, make a simple outline

    - State the main topics with sub-points beneath, leaving plenty of space around each.
    - Beside each point, in a few sentences, write what you want to say.
    - List verses that support each point. Write the entire verse, not just the reference.
    - Highlight, bold or underline the key parts of each verse.
    - If a verse is often misunderstood, add verses before and after to give context.

2. Test yourself

    - Read through your outline and sentences out loud.
    - Is anything missing?
    - Are the supporting Scriptures clear?
    - Can you disprove it?
    - What questions could people ask?
    - Is the explanation concise and simple? Can you make it simple enough to explain to a child?

3. Envision and prepare what you will say

    - Is your explanation the right length of time for the situation? A good test is to imagine explaining to a coworker over break time.
    - Use everyday language, not "Christian-ese." For example, "washed in the blood" might make sense to fellow believers, but may be really disturbing to a non-believer.

- Remember that our goal is not to impress people with a spiritual or intellectual tone. Jesus made it simple; we need to keep it simple.
- Here's a tip: Before sharing what you have learned with someone, take time to try to disprove what you are going to share. This exercise will:
  - Solidify your understanding
  - Prepare you to answer questions

  Remember that, especially when discussing with an unbeliever, we are not aiming to start an argument.

4. When sharing with a person or group
   - Pray for the meeting beforehand.
   - Share with them with love and humility.
   - Consider giving your testimony if it is relevant to the topic.
   - Tell your message. Keep your outline on hand.
   - Deliver your message with humility. Be real, not antagonistic.
   - Summarize key points. Let them know how this truth changed your life.
   - Answer questions but don't be afraid to admit that you don't know.*

*When you don't know the answer to a question, simply say, "Let me get back to you on that point." This is a salesperson's greatest trick to form a relationship — HAVE A REASON TO COME BACK. Take time to solidify yourself on all the points you discussed, then go back and share the answer with them and watch how the Holy Spirit leads your conversation. Encountering difficult questions when sharing the Gospel and finding the answers is a great way to take your Christian walk to a Christian run!

Before ending this section, I would like to share a few tips from my experience (successes *and* failures). If you begin sharing the Bible with people, you will almost assuredly come across people who have hurt, bitterness and anger about certain biblical topics. You may feel like you failed if the person doesn't seem excited or care about what you are saying.

- Don't take a negative response personally.
- Refuse to feel hurt, offended or angry. The best way to keep bitterness away is to earnestly pray for that person.
- Remember that there is only one way to grow: practice. Just as a father and mother cheer for their child when they try to walk or ride a bike for the first time, our Father is cheering us on.
- Don't give up. I can guarantee that the enemy will tempt you to give up sharing Scripture with others. Refuse to quit.
- Don't shrink back or feel embarrassed. God is pleased with you. Don't buy into the lie that your message doesn't matter or that it's silly. Go for it!

"Never give in,
Never give in,
Never, never, never"
Winston Churchill

CLOSING THOUGHTS

Bible study used to be something we did because it was *the right thing to do*, not because we wanted to. The more we studied, the more we wanted to. There is nothing like getting revelation from the Holy Spirit as you read. He is the master communicator, encourager, and revealer of truth.

As you receive revelation from the Holy Spirit, remember that revelation is meant to be shared. One day God showed me that the revelation I receive from the Holy Spirit isn't meant to be stockpiled into my spiritual treasure chest. Every time I would receive revelation, I would joyfully write it into my journal and there it would sit (which really frustrated Kevin). God showed me how Bible teachers have brought me miles ahead of where I would have been by sharing the revelation they had been given. What a gift! The Holy Spirit's revelation to us is not usually meant to be kept a secret. We build up our fellow disciples of Jesus by sharing the truth we have been given in love and humility.

You have been specially made in God's image to share Him with others in a unique way. Yes, you can share the good news of Jesus with others. You have something that no one else has: your personal testimony. You have a unique way of thinking and communicating. You have a group of friends and acquaintances that no one else has. This is a fact: only you can reach people in the way God has equipped you.

You don't need to worry about your particular ministry or spiritual gifts or anointings because you have THE gift: the gift of the Holy Spirit. He is there to enable you do to everything that God has called you to do. God has given every believer the ministry of reconciliation (2 Corinthians 5:18). Our job is to reconcile, or bring, every person to God. We do this by preaching the Gospel and in the process, we heal the sick, raise the dead, cast out demons and more.

God the Father, Jesus Christ and the Holy Spirit are our biggest cheerleaders, encouraging us to reach out to people. People in the world are praying for someone to help them, encourage them, and tell them who God has made them to be. You are the hands and feet of Jesus. Remember that Christ in you is the hope of glory (Colossians 1:27). As we trust Him, He helps us accomplish His will.

Did you notice the second part of Colossians 1:27 "…the hope of glory?" Christ in you is Heaven's hope to reach the world. It was a big revelation to me when I realized that I gave up my right to choose whether to obey God when I made Jesus my Lord (1 Corinthians 6:20). Now that I belong to Him body, soul and spirit, His mission is my mission. It doesn't matter if I feel shy or inadequate, I must be God's ambassador to this world (2 Corinthians 5:20). You belong to Him, too. God has placed His Holy Spirit inside you; His power enables you to do everything He has called you to do. Trust Him, step out of your comfort zone, and be Jesus to this world.

Matthew 28:18-20 — [18] And Jesus came and spoke to them, saying, "All authority has been given to Me in heaven and on earth. [19] Go therefore and make disciples of all the nations, baptizing them in the name of the Father and of the Son and of the Holy Spirit, [20] teaching them to observe all things that I have commanded you; and lo, I am with you always, *even* to the end of the age."

CHRIST IN YOU IS HEAVEN'S HOPE TO REACH THE WORLD.

Bibliography

(2017, March 26). Retrieved from The Webster's Dictionary 1828 - Online Edition: webstersdictionary1828.com

Better Explained. (2017, April 2). Retrieved from Site Philosophy: betterexplained.com/philosophy

BibleGateway.com: A searchable online Bible. (2017, January 5). Retrieved from BibleGateway: biblegateway.com

Blake, C. (2006). *Divine Healing Technician Training (DHT).* Retrieved from John G. Lake Ministries (JGLM): www.jglm.org

Blake, C. (2007). *DBI Year 1 Course 3 - Christian DNA.* Retrieved from Dominion Bible Institute (DBI): Dbi.jglm.org

Fay, W. (1998). *Share Jesus Without Fear: Personal Evangelism New Testament.* B&H Publishing Group.

Liardon, R. (2003). *God's Generals: Why They Succeeded and Why Some Fail.* Whitaker house.

Never Give In (Audio). (2017, March 30). Retrieved from The International Churchill Society: https://www.winstonchurchill.org/resources/speeches/1941-1945-war-leader/never-give-in-harrow-school

Oxford English Dictionary. (2017, January 17). Retrieved from oed.com

Porter, J. (2016, December 15). *Journalistics.com.* Retrieved from Five Ws and One H: The Secret to Complete News Stories: http://blog.journalistics.com/2010/five-ws-one-h/

Strong, J. (2009). *Strong's Exhaustive Concordance of the Bible.* Hendrickson Publishing.

Made in the USA
Middletown, DE
10 May 2022